Acting Strategies
for the Cyber Age

Donated By

Acting Strategies
for the
Cyber Age

Ed Hooks

Heinemann
Portsmouth, NH

Heinemann
A division of Reed Elsevier Inc.
361 Hanover Street
Portsmouth, NH 03801–3912
www.heinemanndrama.com

Offices and agents throughout the world

Library of Congress Cataloging-in-Publication Data
Hooks, Ed.
    Acting strategies for the cyber age / Ed Hooks.
        p. cm.
    Includes bibliographical references.
    ISBN 0-325-00240-1 (pbk.)
    1. Acting. 2. Acting—Computer network resources. I. Title.

    PN2061 .H64 2001
    792'.028—dc21   00-069959

Editor: Lisa A. Barnett
Production: Vicki Kasabian
Cover design: Jenny Jensen Greenleaf
Manufacturing: Steve Bernier

Printed in the United States of America on acid-free paper
05 04 03 02 01 VP 1 2 3 4 5

Contents

When we are all together in Cyberspace then we will see what the human spirit, and the basic desire to connect, can create there. I am convinced that the result will be more benign if we go there open-minded, open-hearted, excited with the adventure, than if we are dragged into exile.

John Perry Barlow, *Utne Reader*

All the world's a stage.

William Shakespeare, *As You Like It*,
Act II, scene vii

Acknowledgments

First, I must thank Lisa Barnett, senior editor of Heinemann, for giving me the opportunity to put in print my perspective on the ancient and honorable art of acting. Financial pressures being what they are in publishing these days, it is not easy to put money on the table when an author begins writing *shaman* and *empathy* in the same sentence as *cyberspace*. A safer bet would be Book Number Ninety-Six on the subject of how to meet casting directors and agents. Ms. Barnett and the editorial staff at Heinemann are people of the theater, and I am proud to be in their company.

Second, I must thank my wife, Cally, always and forever my most incisive critic and cheerleader, and my daughter, Dagny, who shows such marvelous promise as a writer herself.

Director Gregory Burke has been helpful to the process by pointing me toward the latest in digital technology. My good friend Lee Phillips is long overdue for thanks because I have been inspired by our many conversations about the arts. Thanks, too, to Paulo and the expert espresso-pulling staff at Cafe Torrefazione in downtown Palo Alto, California. It was at their front counter that I wrote large portions of this book.

Finally, I want to thank my acting students, past and present. You are the future, and I send you each and every one a sincere cyber hug.

Acting Strategies
for the Cyber Age

Introduction

The cyber age is an exciting time to be an actor. This new century brings with it opportunities that were only a few years ago the stuff of science fiction. As with everything in life that is worthwhile, however, the opportunities come at a cost. Actors will be able to fly higher, bouncing performances off satellites and reaching global audiences, but they can no longer depend on the tried-and-true ways of managing their careers. Hollywood's fabled Schwab's drugstore, where Lana Turner was rumored to have been discovered sitting at the soda fountain, is no more. Time was that aspiring actors would step off the bus in Hollywood, get some headshots taken, and start knocking on talent agency doors. Some will still do that, but it is not enough any more. Some of the most dazzling new venues for actors do not yet pay enough money to motivate the involvement of commission-based agents or uptown casting directors. Actors who rely exclusively on the traditional ways of pursuing a career stand a good chance of being left at the starting gate.

There is forming in the entertainment industry a subculture of cyber-pioneer actors, directors, writers, and producers, a group focused on emerging global audiences, digital technology, the Internet, and audience interactivity. They are telling their stories just as Sophocles did in ancient Greece and Shakespeare did in Elizabethan England, but they are standing on a new kind of stage. The impulse to perform and connect with an audience is the same as it has been for thousands of years, but the *way* the performance is reaching the audience is changing.

The twenty-first-century actor is a pioneer of the sort we have not seen since movies first appeared in the early 1900s. He cannot look to past generations for guidance because they never had to deal with anything like this. Instead, he must orient himself globally, check the direction of sunrise, and hack out his own cyber pathway. At the start of the twentieth century, before Hollywood even had a name, there were few recognizable career road signs for actors. There were no unions, no SAG-franchised talent agencies, no casting directors, and few guidelines of any kind. When Cecil B. DeMille shot *The Squaw Man* in 1914, Los Angeles was a dirt-road town, and he wore a loaded pistol on his hip to discourage competitors from tossing sand into his cameras. It was every person for himself back then because there were no other alternatives, no governing authority. Most movie production was still centered on the East Coast, where hundreds of companies were producing short silent films, just as there are hundreds of companies today producing short digital videos. The Vitograph Company alone was releasing a new movie every three days in 1909. Today, you can visit the website for iFilm (<www.iFilm.com>) and download over 1,500 short films, and the numbers grow weekly. The entertainment industry at the dawn of the twenty-first century is similar in dynamic—if not in particulars—to that of a hundred years ago. It is an environment for the joyful and the adventurous, the dreamers and the visionaries.

There are legal parallels to the old days, too, as Hollywood conglomerates try to restrict and control distribution rights to all things digital. Their attempts at total control mirror Thomas Edison's futile efforts to restrict access to motion picture film stock. The Edison Trust, as it was known, wanted to collect a royalty on every foot of motion picture film manufactured. The strategy didn't work in 1910, and it won't work today. Once a technology is out there in the marketplace and the public gets used to it, it is virtually impossible to turn back the traffic. You can try to set up a tollbooth, but the cars will simply drive around your outstretched hand, which is the kind of situation we see developing now.

This book then is about the future of acting and the past, about digital technology, cyberspace, and storytelling. It is about the concentration of corporate power at the highest levels, the decentralization of storytelling power into the hands of the individual artist, and the impact of all of these changes on the career of new cyber-age actors. Join with me please as I put my finger to the wind and check the direction of the sunrise. The cyber future is waiting, and all bets are off.

"*The More They Stay the Same*"

The Internet and digital technology, combined with high-speed transmission, have expanded the entire entertainment industry in remarkable ways. An actor today must not only know what stage right and stage left are, but also be familiar with the words *bandwidth, browser, interactive,* and *portal.* The digital mini-film, a form that didn't exist until recently, is suddenly all the rage, and there are film festivals organized especially to showcase them. New cyberspace multiplexes like atomfilm.com and iFilm.com seem to pop up almost daily, and a low-budget ($40,000) digital video movie entitled *Blair Witch Project* grossed over $150 million. The Federal Communications Commission is reporting that more Americans are ramping up to DSL (digital subscriber line) and ISDN access speed on their computers, which makes it possible to download live-action and animated films almost instantly without the herky-jerky quality that was the plague of horse-and-buggy 28.8 BPS modems. Wait lists for these high-speed connections are months long in some parts of the country.

In 1950, when Marlon Brando was a young actor, barely 10 percent of Americans owned television sets and the first television network was just two years old. Commercial residuals, which today represent the largest percentage of the average SAG actor's income, didn't yet exist. Fiber optics was unknown. Actors worked almost exclusively in the legitimate theatre, making occasional forays into movies and then retreating once again to the stage. Ground Zero was New York, not Hollywood. An actor in those days did not dare spend too much time in front of cameras lest he be perceived by his peers to be selling out, compromising his integrity. Movies were considered by most actors to be low-ball entertainment aimed at the masses, not an art form for the discerning patron.

Technology is developing now at such a breakneck pace, in fact, that entirely new platforms for acting may appear at any time. There is a growing demand for visual storytelling of all kinds, in feature form, short form, computer games, and commercials. The era of low-budget and no-budget personal filmmaking is here. Compliments of the Internet, new global theatrical communities are forming and previously undetected audiences are appearing. Analog videotape, barely twenty-five years old, is on its way out and digital is in. Within the next ten years, DVDs and CD-ROMs will probably be replaced by something else, and the person who wants to enjoy a movie or stage play will be able to click a few buttons and see whatever she wants. What is more, she will see it whenever she wants, in high definition, in her living room or on a portable screen she carries around with her. She will increasingly have the option of being entertained passively or interactively. She will be able to watch the show or be a virtual character in it.

Power has been the hot commodity of the twentieth-century entertainment industry, and in the cyber age power is shifting in two directions at once. On the corporate end, it is being consolidated through mergers and acquisitions into the hands of five huge multinational entertainment conglomerates: News Corporation (Fox), Viacom, Sony, AOL Time-Warner, Seagram, and Disney. Together, those five companies control virtually all of mainstream Hollywood movie production, movie theatres (exhibition), and network and cable television. They produce the programs and then exhibit them in a closed-shop kind of way. The big story of the early twenty-first century, however, is that digital technology is shifting the power of actual storytelling downward, into the hands of the individual artist, and the audiences are starting to enjoy programming-on-demand. For example, two companies (TiVo and ReplayTV) brought to market in 1999 devices that allow a television viewer to personalize his programming. By hooking up a device made by one of these companies and properly programming it, he can watch what he wants, when he wants to watch it. Remarkably, this technology allows the viewer to pause live programming, like the evening news or a football game, replaying it a moment later and even skipping commercials! The consumer can break free of the preset air schedule of television networks to create his own roster of programming, in essence, his own network.

Other major companies, like AT&T, are experimenting with devices that will compete with TiVo and Replay TV. Within a few years, this is most likely how television watchers will be watching television, and there will be a dramatic change in the way networks generate advertising revenues. Personal television is going to change the way networks advertise now that airtime becomes fluid and flexible and demographics fall by the wayside.

Digital technology and the Internet are free to anybody who wants to use them. Try though they will, the Big Five will be unable to alter the flow of this mighty river. Their frustration, already palpable, is moving into the political arena. Just as they tried to pass laws outlawing the development of the VCR in the 1980s, they are trying to pass laws now restricting the evolution of digital. One almost wants to feel sorry for the Old Guard. The traditional world of Hollywood moguldom is being turned upside down, and they seriously do not know what to do about it. AOL, the largest Internet Service Provider (ISP), recently acquired movie/TV/publishing behemoth Time-Warner. You can go ahead and put an asterisk next to that last sentence because it represents a milestone in entertainment industry history. AOL bought Time-Warner, not the other way around. The earth has moved. Push has come to shove. Hell must have frozen over.

Telling Stories

One thing, however, is not changing, nor will it ever: After you take away the cyber bells and whistles, the actor still stands on a stage and he will still communicate with the audience. Regardless of who owns Time-Warner, the transaction between actor and audience that has been going on for thousands of years is the underlying value. It may be pushed into cyberspace and digitized, and the audience may physically disappear from the immediate view of the actor, but the transaction itself remains the same. This fact of life is why, regardless of how complicated the entertainment industry becomes in the cyber age, power must trickle down to the artist. Actors are the primary storytellers, and nobody is going very far without them. Some will try, as the TV networks did with the "reality shows," which appeared in the summer of 2000 (remember *Survivor* and *Big Brother*?), but the public's need for storytelling runs deep. Throughout history, we have learned our most fundamental lessons about life through stories. If the television networks were to schedule wall-to-wall reality programs, the move would only encourage the appearance of new venues for actors. When it comes to matters of the heart, it is bedrock fact that the more things change, the more they stay the same.

Drama is about storytelling. Whether we're talking about Oedipus and his mom, Tom Winfield and his mom, or Hamlet and his mom, it's all storytelling and is designed to make a point. Throughout history, from ancient Greece and earlier, right up through Shakespeare's England and Molière's France, the actor has always been the primary storyteller. In the mid-twentieth century, however, the situation began to change. As the production of motion pictures became a glamorous and popular industry, the actor began to be pushed aside in favor of the auteur movie director. Mainstream acting training began to focus on teaching actors how to stimulate themselves emotionally rather than to tell stories. A well-trained actor would come to be defined as a person of strong body and voice who is emotionally accessible, sensitive to direction, and highly castable.

Actors today face three primary challenges. First, there are some among us who are intimidated by all of these high-tech developments. I have friends—good theatre people, mainly over forty years of age—whose eyes glaze over whenever the conversation shifts to the subject of the Internet. Rather than see the potential in broadband communication, they feel a threat. In their view, acting is a kind of zero sum game. A gain for cyber space is a loss for the legitimate theatre. That is incorrect, of course, but it's easy to empathize with their fears. Actors are a touchy-feely group, and all of this Internet talk is the opposite of that. It's left-brain versus right-brain stuff.

The second challenge is that many actors have either not learned or have forgotten that acting is storytelling. It has been bred out of them by our lowest common denominator, pop culture. If you ask a new actor today why he wants to act, he is likely to become tongue-tied. He doesn't know why; he only knows that he wants to. Like a thoroughbred horse that comes to favor the racetrack over the meadow, many actors today are disoriented and disconnected from themselves. They have the impulse to perform, but it is not in the service of the story or the community. Instead, it is for self-validation. Acting for some has become an elixir for delivering up psychic visibility in a complex, alienating culture and Andy Warhol's fifteen minutes of fame.

Finally, some aspiring actors have no idea what is required of them in terms of training if they are to have a career in the arts. Again, the confusion is easy to understand because they have been raised on a diet of television shows that feature casts comprised of sports figures, stand-up comics, and models as often as actual actors. Then, when they begin searching for acting training, they find the choices bewildering.

The United States is a society that does not enthusiastically support the arts, which is why acting as an art form is not widely understood. Actors are forced to spend far too much of their time searching for work instead of acting. We have an imbalanced system of supply and demand in the entertainment industry. There are many more applicants than there are job vacancies for actors. Actors are continually placed in a low-status posture in the marketplace. "Pul-eeeze cast me!" we implore, assuming a subservient posture time and again. This dynamic is antithetical to that of the actor-as-shaman, the actor-as-storyteller, and the actor-as-leader. Cyber-age technology promises to reempower the actor.

In my acting classes, I routinely ask new students if they are actors now or if they hope to be actors some day. If they say they hope to be actors some day, I explain that they have a problem. I cannot snap my fingers and turn a person into an actor. I cannot teach acting to someone who wants to be an actor some day. I can only help the person who already considers himself to be an actor to become a better actor. No teacher—and this includes Constantin Stanislavsky and Lee Strasberg and the entire roster of contemporary teachers—can make an actor out of someone who does not already consider himself to be one. This points to the paradox in many acting schools. The traditional relationship between student and teacher is one in which the teacher leads and the student follows. But acting doesn't work like that. When it comes to acting, the student must lead from the very first moment. The teacher may lead in lecture and notes on scenes, but the actor must take high status when he is performing. Unfortunately, many acting teachers thrive emotionally and financially by keeping the student actor in a subservient position, which is what leads to the acting-teacher-as-guru syndrome and turns some people into perpetual students instead of actors.

The burden is on the teacher to create an atmosphere in the workshop that allows the student to lead when he is on stage. Stanislavsky himself enunciated the challenge in *My Life in Art*: "Without talent or ability one must not go on the stage. In our organized schools of dramatic art it is not so today. What they need is a certain quantity of paying pupils. And not everyone who can pay has talent or can hope to become an actor" (Stanislavsky 1925, 79).

A new actor arrives on the scene at one of the most exciting moments in theatrical history, but he's stuck in a conundrum. He feels in his gut that he wants to act, but he doesn't feel qualified and doesn't know how to proceed. He wants the validation of training, but he doesn't know which training is necessary or which teachers are best. He feels the impulse to lead, but that conflicts with the evident necessity that he follow, first in school and then in pursuit of employment.

There is an overabundance of information in cyberspace delivered to the consumer/citizen at a speed that is much too fast for many people to keep up with. It is easy to feel isolated, left behind, and alienated in the twenty-first century. The tribe has lost its form, and families are scattered across continents. A person of fragile self-esteem might conclude that there is power in the visual image itself. If one manages to get one's image onto a movie or television screen, then one's life *must* be meaningful, right? Seeing is believing. The impulse that brings such a person to acting is distorted and focused inward on the self rather than outward on the audience. Consequently, some aspiring actors are skipping the legitimate theatre altogether. They see no point in the stage because they are not thinking about audiences in the amphitheatre or Globe sense of the word. They are lured by the prospect of fame, celebrity, and acceptance, and they easily find acting schools that will cater to this orientation. Jean Smart, a respected, award-winning, stage-trained veteran actor of movies and television, was interviewed in connection with the opening of a new Broadway show. When asked about her experiences in Hollywood, she said, "I was stunned when I came to L.A. [at the] number of actors I met who had never done theatre. I actually didn't know that such people existed. I really didn't. I didn't get it" (*San Francisco Examiner*, 19 August 2000). Carey Perloff, Artistic Director of San Francisco's American Conservatory Theatre, shook her artistic head over the same issue in another interview: "After this cadre of actors, it's over. Actors today may start in the theatre, but they find themselves in TV and film eventually" (*San Jose Mercury News*, 2 July 2000).

The time is ripe . . . correction: the time is *urgent* for the actor to reassess why he acts. The twenty-first-century actor must not only carry the torch forward but must decide where to carry it. Because he will be spending most of his time in front of cameras, acting for audiences that are invisible to him, and because much of his acting will be frankly in the service of commerce instead of art, it will be increasingly easy to feel artistically disoriented. The danger is that the shamanistic torch might dim.

Your Acting Roots

Becoming a professional actor is like getting called to the priesthood. It requires an act of faith and a commitment, and is not something you work out with your college counselor or career mentor. You don't take an aptitude test and narrow down your career choices to, say, forest ranger, tennis pro, or actor. It is true that once the decision is made, there are steps you can take to properly prepare yourself, but you don't enter a career as an actor in a conventional way. As is the case with all arts, acting is an irrational thing to be doing for a living. The odds against financial success—no, even financial survival—are overwhelming. Eighty-five percent of the members of Screen Actors Guild earn less than five thousand dollars per year from acting, and half the people that come into acting get right back out within three years because they can't make enough to live on. None of this matters a whit to a person who knows that he simply must act. For the true actor, there are no other alternatives worthy of consideration.

Do you remember the moment you decided to become an actor? For me, it happened in Baltimore, Maryland, in 1968, at the Mechanic Theatre. After the curtain fell on a national touring company production of *Cabaret* and the audience cleared the auditorium, I remained in my seat and watched from the shadows as the stagehands reset props for the next show. Their quiet efficiency enthralled me; something about it said to me, "Here is magic." As I sat there in my businessman suit, I suddenly longed more than anything to be part of the theatrical family, to rip those pinstripes off and help make the magic. I decided then and there that I wanted to be an actor, and the next day I gave notice to my employer that I was quitting.

During the weeks following my decision, I discovered that I was self-conscious and embarrassed by the commitment I was making. I resisted telling anybody about it except my wife. Who was I to presume I could act, after all? What made me think I had the stuff to succeed? What did success as an actor really mean? Why did I have this longing anyway? The truth is, at that point I wasn't thinking about succeeding, and I didn't have a clue why I was so drawn to the theatre.

11

Those first urges to act had nothing to do with getting paid any more than a person who has been called to the priesthood first thinks of having a parish of his own. One would live . . . somehow. The lifestyle is what drew me, along with the prospect of making theatrical magic.

Actors love to talk about their early experiences with acting. Frequently, the memories are of high school or college plays. Maybe the role was Abigail in *The Crucible* or Henry Drummond in *Inherit the Wind* or Viola in *Twelfth Night*. Whatever it was, the experience was carefree. Acting in school plays is as close as the modern actor gets to a tribal experience. It is an innocent kind of thing. Nobody in the cast has yet seriously studied acting, and the basic idea is to have fun. Nobody has yet had any talent agency doors slammed in his face. The audience bonds with the actors in a very familiar, a loving, and, frequently, a family way. From start to finish, it is a community activity, with all that implies.

So why *did* you become an actor? What was the incident that pushed you over the line from dreaming into doing? Just as the moment of inspiration is a special memory for a priest, so too is this one for you. If you discussed with your family your decision to act, the announcement was probably not celebrated and may well have caused heated debate. You made the commitment anyway because acting was your imperative and your dream, and for that alone you deserve a prolonged round of applause. During your career, you will encounter plenty of rejection, and it is a good thing to stay connected with the moment of inspiration. It will give you comfort.

From Shamans to Boards to Cyberspace

Before there were movies or television, there was stage. Before there were stages made from concrete and steel, there were stages built of wood. Before there was stages built of wood, there was stages stamped into the dirt. Before there was distance between the actor and the audience, the performing arena was defined by a circle drawn in that dirt, around which the tribe gathered. If you want to understand the true roots of the actor's craft, you have to dig deeper than Greek theatre and the emergence of Thespis. You have to go back several thousand years earlier, to shamanism.

Seven thousand years ago, those individuals that were able to act were considered special and were held in high esteem by their communities and tribes. By the time we got into the nineteenth century, however, actors had fallen from grace. We became second-class citizens, transients, and bad credit risks. Ever see a picture of that famous rooming-house sign, "No Actors or Dogs Allowed"? That's no joke. Ever have someone remind you that it was an actor who killed Abe Lincoln? It may be a funny joke, but the truth is that nobody really wants their kid to marry an actor, and few parents wish for their kid that he become an actor. If you mention *acting* at a party and ask for associative words, you'll hear *celebrity*, *fame*, *television*, *movies*, maybe *stage*, not *artist*, *teacher*, or *shaman*.

Shamans were the first actors. They were used by their tribes to communicate with the animal spirits and calm the weather so as to assure a productive hunt, and they helped heal the sick. Survival in those primitive days was a negotiation with the elements and wild animals, and the tribe could use all the help it could get. Shamans, therefore, filled an important function. They helped the tribe believe in itself. They helped its members believe they could make it through another rough winter. When the shaman did his job, he said to the tribe in effect, "Come with me. I will take you on a spiritual journey. When you get back, you will feel better about yourself, and the hunt will be fruitful." Think about it for a moment: Isn't that ancient transaction very much like what happens in the modern-day theatre? Isn't the actor who portrays Blanche Dubois or Willy Loman still saying, "Come with me. I will take you on a journey. When you get back, you will feel better about yourself"? The twenty-first-century actor has much in common with his shaman ancestors.

There are certain contemporary fundamentalist religions in which worshippers speak in tongues and are moved by the spirit. The faithful may leap around and even roll in the church aisles. Despite this physical and verbal abandon, they are in control of what they are doing. I saw a documentary about these religions once and was impressed that the devoted were both "taken over" and in control. To me, that is almost a direct parallel to what actors know as "transformation," the feeling that the character seems to be dictating the movement and words, and yet the actor is still in control. This fits with the idea of actor-as-shaman. "The shaman is a 'master of spirits' who performs in trance, primarily for the purpose of curing the sick by ritualistic means" (Kirby 1975, 1). "In ritual as in drama the aim is an enhanced level of consciousness, a memorable insight into the nature of existence" (Esslin 1976, 28).

It is important to note where those early shamans come from. It's not like there were random bands of nomadic shamans who dropped in for tribal house calls. There were no shaman schools or shaman casting directors. Probably then as now, there were those members of the tribe that seemed more sensitive than most. These people were more in touch with the dream world and animal spirits and they felt called to perform. Individuals who seemed to be special in this way were singled out, pushed forward, and encouraged. The important point is that shamanism was from the start an integral part of tribal life, and the role of the shaman was important. The tribe needed something that only a shaman could deliver. Then as now, not everybody was cut out to be an actor. Some people make better soldiers or cooks. Only the most charismatic and powerful person would be a shaman and inspire the trust of the tribe.

By the fifth century B.C. in Greece—the starting point from which we in the West usually measure acting and drama—shamanism had given way to a more organized tribal ritual called a *dithyramb*. A dithyramb is a hymn sung in unison, involving a chorus of fifty men, five from each of the tribes of Attica. The chorus gathered during special festivals around an altar of Dionysius and sang songs about demigods, people who were part god and part human. At the City Dionysia, "the dramatic spectacle was one of the rituals that deliberately aimed at maintaining social identity and reinforcing the cohesion of the group" (Longo 1990, 10). After Thespis stepped forward and began to talk back to the chorus, the dithyramb stopped being a chant and became instead a dialogue. (Yes, that is where the word *thespian* came from.) The focus of the festivals shifted away from man's relationship with the gods and onto man's relationship with man. Actors began to portray human characters and interacted in structured dramas that made a thematic point.

Role-playing began in ancient Greece it's true, but role-playing was just another development in the age-old way tribes communicated with themselves. First came shamans, then came role-playing actors. The common denominator was communication, which is precisely the foundation of the impulse to act in the cyber age. Across nine thousand years of history, nothing has fundamentally changed. As was the case with early shamans, actors still reach out and touch the tribe. But if actors are still shamans, where is the tribe? For whom do we act? What is the tribal common good in the cyber age? Does anybody really need a shaman any more?

For the first shamans, there was no separation at all between performer and audience. Beginning with that circle drawn in the dirt, the actor's arena has expanded through history. At first, he played for tribesmen who were only inches away, literally close enough to touch. For the earliest Greeks (before Thespis), "there was no split or distinction between the stage area and the auditorium, nor between the actors and the public—that is, the community" (Longo 1990, 16). By the time the amphitheatre was built in ancient Greece, the spectator had moved into the seats, and the actor took a playing area. By Shakespeare's day, actors were seen on a wooden stage and, by the seventeenth century, footlights appeared, accentuating the distance between actors and audience. The proscenium arch followed, literally framing the action of the play and further enunciating the distance between actor and audience. Today, we have multimedia and cameras. The audience can be measured in the millions of people, and they are removed from the actor's work by space and mechanical replay.

John Guare noted in his widely produced play, *Six Degrees of Separation,* that each person in the world is connected to all the other people in the world by no more than six levels of connection. In other words, you have a friend or relative who has a friend or relative who has a friend or relative who has a friend or relative who has a friend or relative who is a friend or relative to the President of the United States. You're also that far removed from the Pope and whatever murderers are sitting on death row in Texas. It is a fascinating statistic and concept. What it really means is that we are all connected—and yet, we are strangers. Scientists tell us that all humans are 99.9 percent identical if measured by DNA. We're all in the same tribe, and yet we are isolated. A community may experience itself as a community at church on Sunday, but theatre, a place where the tribe has gathered throughout history, rarely serves that function any more. That warm and fuzzy feeling that fills the high school auditorium when the lights come up on *Our Town* or *The Music Man* is not evident on the set of a Hollywood situation comedy. Few people in a studio audience know one another, and tribal joy is indicated by the insertion of a prerecorded laugh track.

A person who is inspired to become an actor today may still be special in that shamanistic way. He may be more sensitive than his peers, and he may feel a greater sensitivity to things spiritual and psychological. He may proudly and expectantly step toward that circle in the dirt, but unlike his shaman ancestors, he is not chosen. The tribe still has spiritual needs, but it is out of touch with itself and does not know where to look for comfort and answers. It does not recognize that the actor can help in this regard. We have churches and synagogues, but these institutions are based on man's relationship to God. To the degree that they teach about man's relationship with man, it is only to be in the service of God. We have psychiatrists and psychologists for those who can afford them, and we have self-help counselors and gurus of all kinds. But the actor—the person in history most entrusted with the task of telling stories about mankind—has been made into a cultural amusement. A new actor is not led to believe that his contribution to the tribe is essential at all. An actor today is in fact more isolated from the community than are his brothers and sisters who choose careers as lawyers, doctors, and business executives.

French philosopher Denis Diderot pointed out two hundred years ago that the stage is a pulpit. I agree and frequently cite his words in my own acting classes. When I do, I can detect an immediate shift in the group dynamic. It is as if the modern actor has this reptilian brain, with a deeply buried sense of his shamanistic self. He knows on some primitive and long-forgotten level that the stage is his natural realm and that there is something vaguely spiritual about it. Rather than being proud of his calling, however, he has been conditioned in our society to feel shame at wanting to "show off." Rather than being nurtured as an artist, he has been mildly rebuked by the community he would serve. Like Rosencrantz and Guildenstern, he has dutifully made the trip, but he has no idea why he was summoned.

The dawn of the cyber age is the perfect time for actors to reconnect with their shaman roots. Since actors cannot look to the tribe for a measure of their moral worth, they must look over their shoulders and into the distant past. Acting is an honorable thing to do with your life. The world needs shamans more now than it ever has. If the tribe does not honor you, it is not because you as an actor are unimportant, but because the tribe has forgotten how to hold up the mirror to its own self. It has forgotten what shamans are for. It is up to you to remind them.

Prelude to an Acting Career

Preparation for an acting career begins a long time before you enroll in acting classes or pose for a headshot. Acting is an interpretative art, a communication between minds, and that means the artist must have something to say. Whether we are talking about a play, a painting, a movie, or a symphony, audience and artist are communicating. It is a truism that there is no such thing as a dumb good actor, and that is why the best actors have a strong general education and a definite point of view. A compelling actor is one who is always learning things, always paying attention to life and to human interaction. Shakespeare advises in *Hamlet* that the actor should hold the mirror up to nature, and that means the actor must be a good student of human nature. Learning your lines and saying them truthfully are a minor part of what is going on when you act.

Before we explore what is necessary to be a good actor, however, let's consider for a moment the creative contributions of other people who are involved in a theatrical production. A play or a movie is obviously a collaborative undertaking involving a director and a playwright (or screenwriter) in addition to the actors and technical crew. If interpretative art involves communication between minds, then plays and movies have a lot of different people doing some communicating, right? This is an important point. Shamans were the original primary storytellers. There were no other parties involved except for the shaman and the tribe. In Shakespeare's day, there were large casts of actors and playwrights but no directors at all. The playwrights sort of doubled as directors, suggesting within the text how a play ought to be staged. Directors first appeared during the nineteenth century and, by the twentieth century, became celebrity artists in their own rights. There are many different people involved in a theatrical production, and each of them can argue that his is the primary artistic vision. Particularly in the United States, there has been a lot of discussion and disagreement on this point. Movies are generally considered to be a director's medium, and the stage is still considered an actor's medium, but neither of these assertions is bedrock correct. Before we go further, let's consider the most widely held opinions. Having a firm grasp on this concept of who is the primary storyteller can help light your way.

When I went to acting school in the late sixties, I was taught to serve the play. That is, that the actor's job is to figure out what the playwright is trying to say and then to help him say it. I do not recall a single teacher during those days at New York's American Academy of Dramatic Arts mentioning to me that I might be a primary artist or a storyteller, or that my point of view was worth sharing. I was to be a conduit for the playwright. This perspective fits well with that of playwright David Mamet, who says that "the actor's [job] is to open the mouth, stand straight, and say the words bravely—adding nothing, denying nothing" (Mamet 1999, 22). When I began working as a professional actor, I quickly discovered that not all actors were so respectful of the playwright's intent. One of my first major real-world acting lessons came about when an actress with whom I was cast in summer stock absolutely refused to play her role the way the playwright wrote it. She made it her own, saying the words the playwright wrote but veering a mile away from what the playwright intended her role to convey. I learned that, unless I wanted to look bad on stage, I had to deal with the reality of what she was doing rather than what I thought she ought to be doing or what the playwright had even intended. I disagree, therefore, with Mamet's take on the actor's role in a theatrical production. If actors merely open their mouths and say the words, we have a paradigm for the writer-as-auteur and that's not how things are in the real world. The actor clearly has a mind of his own and a point of view. Under Mamet's scheme, the actor becomes a color in the playwright's palette.

Constantin Stanislavsky honored the playwright at the Moscow Art Theatre, but he also overtly acknowledged the creative role of the actor. Significantly, when Stanislavsky was directing a show, he would have each actor stand up at rehearsal and tell the story of the play. He wanted the actors to be united as storytellers, working in conjunction with a playwright and a director. He did not want an actor to focus only on his own role, to the exclusion of other considerations in the play. Lee Strasberg, the man who invented Method Acting in the United States and was cofounder of the Actor's Studio, departed from Stanislavsky's focus. He taught that the director of a production is the primary storyteller and that the actors should serve the director's vision. "In contrast to Stanislavsky's sense of the actor's freedom as artist, Strasberg's attitude puts artistic control in the hands of the director" (Carnicke 1998, 165). This view of the actor's function was timely because movies were becoming a major pop culture art form in the 1950s. The auteur director was a creation of the movies because, in a movie, production is carried out on a scene-by-scene basis over a long period of time with the director calling all the shots. On stage, by contrast, the curtain goes up, and the actors are out there in front of the audience until the curtain comes down. Actors on the legitimate stage are more obviously in charge of the primary theatrical transaction. This is probably why the Actor's Studio produced so many notable movie actors during its heyday.

It is significant and troubling that both Mamet and Strasberg, two major lights of twentieth-century American theatre, are in conflict with Stanislavsky's perception of the actor as a primary storyteller. Stanislavsky is, after all, the father of modern acting. I contend that this thinking is not only out of step with Stanislavsky but with the longer history of acting as an art form that is rooted in shamanism. The cyber-age actor is poised to reclaim his position as a shaman. Indeed, I contend it essential that he do so. A theatrical production ought to be truly collaborative, with director and playwright joining with the actor to tell the story. It is demeaning to the actor if his only function is to serve the interpretative art of someone else. I am convinced that this shift away from the actor as a respected storyteller is largely responsible for the general low-status position of the actor/artist in late twentieth-century United States culture.

Engaging with the World

The best way a new actor can prepare for a career in the arts is to engage with the world. Pay attention to small events as well as big ones, ask stupid questions, debate contentious issues, vote in elections. Make it your policy neither to hide from the truth nor to rationalize it. Be wary of political correctness. It is good not to offend people in the world, but good art always cuts against the grain.

Read challenging books, including those about acting, but remember that life is learned best through direct experience. Buckminster Fuller, philosopher and inventor of the geodesic dome, encouraged his students and readers to be generalists rather than specialists in life, and I think that is particularly good advice for actors. Go to the opera and ballet; take a class in logic; visit Rome and Paris; invest in a telescope. A good actor is naturally autodidactic. Read the *New York Times* as well as novels by Hemingway, Victor Hugo, and Aristotle's *Poetics*. See as many plays as you can, because you will learn much more about acting from watching a play than you will from watching a movie. In the theatre, the transaction between actor and audience is clear, with all parties breathing the same air and attending to one another on a moment-to-moment basis.

Develop strong opinions, but don't pursue controversy for its own sake. It is not necessary to sit in at nuclear power plants or picket the sale of animal-fur jackets to establish that you have opinions, although there is nothing wrong if you do it. An artist can be extremely private in his views if he wants to. The important thing is that you have the strength of your convictions and that you have a point of view. Great artists throughout history have had strong convictions and many of them have suffered because of them. Try to think of an artist of note in any field whose life would be painted in pastels. Van Gogh? Picasso? Mozart? O'Neill? Virginia Wolff? Charlie Chaplin? Fra Angelico? Masaccio? Eleanor Duse? Tennessee Williams? Molière? Hemingway? Marlon Brando? When you act, you are expressing your opinion about the character you are portraying. You are, in other words, exposing yourself and wearing your values on your sleeve.

Monet and Van Gogh saw the same flower garden, but each had his own point of view about what was important in the flowers. When you admire a Van Gogh painting of a garden, you are communing with the artist. It's the same with actors. When you portray a character, you are saying to the audience, "I understand this about this person." When the audience applauds, it is saying to you, "I see what you mean. I never looked at it that way before," or "I have felt that way myself." It is your mind that is validated, your thoughts, your opinions and point of view. This is why a person will go to see many productions of *Hamlet*. Certainly after the first couple of shows, he knows what the story is, right? He will still see a new production of a great play because he wants to know what this actor thinks makes Hamlet tick, as opposed to what the last actor thought made Hamlet tick. With all due respect to David Mamet, an actor is more than a blank piece of paper on which a playwright writes and, with due respect to Lee Strasberg, he is more than a color for the director's brush. An actor is a primary artist.

Developing a Ten-Year Plan

What do you want to be doing ten years from now? Acting in movies? Acting on stage? Living in Paris? If you crank up your car and don't have a destination, you'll drive around aimlessly. The same applies to your acting career, now more than ever before. Actors are notoriously bad long-range planners, which is partly why we have so much difficulty getting credit at the bank. You cannot afford to march blindly into the future. You have more variables to contend with in the cyber age than did actors a generation ago. Actors too often live for the immediate moment—the lusty applause and instant gratification. The truth is, however, that your career, like start-ups in other industries, deserves a long-range business plan.

Sit down with a legal pad and pencil and let your imagination run wild. Jot down how you would like your life to be ten years from now. Don't worry about what is possible or likely. Just fantasize. If you could snap your fingers and create a life for yourself, what would it include? Broadway? Television? Children? Lots of money? How many and how much?

Once you have done that, write down how you want your life to be five years from now. The thought process is this: "If I want to create my fantasy life by ten years from now, what must be accomplished by five years from now?" With five-year goals, you can be just a bit more earthbound than you were with the ten-year goals, but keep in mind these are goals, destinations. Resist the temptation of dismissing goals as unrealistic. Success and failure are self-fulfilling prophesies. Plan success.

After your five-year goals are on paper, start working backward toward the present, one year at a time. In order to be where you want to be five years from now, what must you have accomplished by four years from now? Three years from now? Next year? Six months from now?

If you are doing everything you can to reach your goals, you will be as happy as it is possible for you to be short of actually being there. If, on the other hand, you know what your goals are and you are not doing everything you can to get there, you'll feel bad about yourself. I would much prefer to see you develop long-range goals that you must address daily and weekly than to see you wandering blithely down the street, hoping some nice casting director will put you in something. Take control of your career and your own destiny!

One more note about goal setting. Every six months sit down with a fresh pad and pencil and go through this exercise again. Make new goals if needed. The likelihood is that your goals will not change, but you want to allow for shifting contexts in your life. You may meet Mister Right and decide to move having children closer to the present in your overall scheme, for instance. Setting long-range goals is a wonderful thing to do, but you don't want to allow those goals to become a grim taskmaster. You should reexamine your goals now and then just to make sure you still hold the same values and desires. Life is, after all, about change.

Making It Happen

You're going to need acting training. It doesn't matter if you train while simultaneously going to auditions and accepting acting work, or if you train first and then pursue the auditions later. Those are both decisions that depend on your age, gender, family situation, geographical location, and goals. A wise person told me once that it doesn't matter what shape your boat is, just as long as it floats. Regardless of how you structure the next ten years of your life, you're going to need acting training. Proviso: Yes, there are some actors who have never stepped foot into an acting class and evidently are possessed of inborn talent and abilities. Based on interviews I have read with them, neither Susan Sarandon nor Sissy Spacek have formally studied acting. Neither has Gary Busey. No matter. It is the very rare actor who will not profit from training. The odds against actors are already so daunting that it only makes sense to arrive on the scene at least well trained. Rather than emulate the few exceptions, I suggest you follow in the footsteps of an artist like Anthony Hopkins (Royal Academy of

Dramatic Art), a serious student early in his career, a teacher for us all later. Meryl Streep (Vassar and Yale Drama School) and Robin Williams (Juilliard) are two other commendable role models.

Acting at the professional level, like playing football in the Super Bowl or tennis at Wimbleton, is a high-stress business. It requires extreme concentration and discipline, positive mental attitude, a responsive body, and emotional sensitivity. Mozart's instrument was the piano. Pavarotti's instrument is his voice. Your actor's instrument is your body. If you want to be able to play a variety of roles, you will need to be physically fit, be emotionally accessible, have a strong voice, and be able to call on acting techniques quickly. In other words, you have to know how to approach a role and how to develop it to performance within the limits of rehearsal—or the lack of it. (A big difference between acting on stage and acting in movies is that in movies, there is very little rehearsal.)

When I started my acting career, I enrolled full-time in a New York acting school, where I took daily or weekly classes in voice, movement, dance, mime, speech, singing, and scene study. If I were starting out today, I would have to add acting-for-camera to that list, plus general classes in film production. And of course, if I were not already computer literate, I would have to take computer classes.

You certainly cannot go wrong with any kind of dance training, even if you don't aspire to being a dancer. It is no mystery to me why NFL football players enroll in ballet classes off-season. That kind of training not only strengthens your muscles but also tunes up your physical impulses. Other possibilities would be martial arts training or Pilates or mime. Yoga is marvelous training. Constantin Stanislavsky wrote in *My Life in Art* that an actor's training in nineteenth-century Russia began with ballet school. Until the formation of the Moscow Art Theatre, there were no acting schools as such in Russia, and so the students who first excelled at ballet were later trained to act via apprenticeship and mentoring arrangements in theatre companies (Stanislavsky 1925, 78–79).

Voice lessons are essential for all actors. If you have a regional accent, you should work privately with a coach to acquire a standard American accent. (I had to temper my southern accent when I started in New York.) Singing lessons will help you learn correct voice placement and will give you stronger breath control. This will come in very handy when you act in plays by Shakespeare or Shaw.

Acting-for-camera training is necessary because the cyber-age actor will be spending so much time in front of cameras. True, you can pick up these skills on the job, but take it from me, please: You will save yourself a lot of time if you enroll in a good camera class early in your career.

Workshops in film production are useful because today's actor has the opportunity to make her own movies. As we'll discuss later (see the Career Strategies chapter), you can buy everything you need to make a low-budget movie now for less than $50,000. That includes a digital video camera and a computer equipped with powerful editing software.

The centerpiece of your training is, of course, scene study. Sometimes known as "technique," scene study is where you get hands-on experience with acting. This is where you learn what to do if you have to portray a psychopath or have to cry on cue. It is not easy to pick a good acting class. When you begin looking for acting teachers, you'll discover that there are a lot of them out there, and the quality varies wildly. If you opt for university training, the choice of specific teachers will largely be made for you but, if you select professional-level private classes, you'll have some big decisions to make. Unfortunately, it is possible to do actual harm to yourself as an actor if you are studying with a teacher who is wrong for you.

How to Select the Best Acting Training

You'll have to choose between university-level, theatre-major programs and private-studio, professional-level training. There are arguments for and against both. The factors that will most strongly influence your choice are your own personal situation and long-term goals. Are you married? How old are you? Do you have a family dependent on you financially? Do you live in a remote area? Are you prepared to move to the Big City? Are you a man or a woman? (See the section in the next chapter entitled Ladies, Can We Talk?)

If you are in your teens or early twenties and have the time and money to do it, a good liberal arts education with a major in theatre is probably the best way to go. If, on the other hand, you are pushing thirty, then it doesn't make much sense to spend four to eight years in college drama programs before making a professional commitment to acting. If you are ready to seek representation and begin auditioning immediately, then professional classes may be best.

There are many good liberal arts colleges in the United States, and a handful of them have drama departments with excellent reputations. A partial list would be New York University (<www.nyu.edu>), University of California Los Angeles (<www.ucla.edu>), Carnegie-Mellon (<www.cmu.edu>), Northwestern University (<www.north western.edu>), and Columbia University (<www.columbia.edu>). A top-notch, full-time, specialized acting program is offered by the Juilliard School of Drama (<www.juilliard.edu>), but admission is very competitive; only 8 percent of applicants are accepted. North Carolina School of the Arts (<www.ncarts.edu>) also has a good program and accepts 47 percent of its applicants.

If you opt for university training, do so with one eye on the possibility of grad school. The Yale School of Drama (<www.yale.edu>) and the NYU Tisch School of Drama (<www.nyu.edu>) offer outstanding graduate-level programs, and graduates there have a strategic advantage over the hoards of actors who get off the bus in New York or L.A. each day. Higher-echelon entertainment-industry talent agents and casting directors always keep an eye on Yale and Tisch graduates, and it is definitely to your advantage to be immediately represented by the "A-list" agents if possible. We'll get into that subject in Career Strategies.

You might consider a one- or two-year program at a private specialty school such as the Neighborhood Playhouse in New York City, American Conservatory Theatre in San Francisco, Goodman Theatre in Chicago, or The American Academy of Dramatic Arts in New York. The argument in favor of these schools is that you will devote your whole day to the study of acting, dance, singing, movement, and so on. The argument against these schools is that you will devote your whole day to the study of acting, dance, singing, movement, and so forth. There is something to be said for a broad-base liberal arts program that includes philosophy, literature, and history.

If I were managing your acting career, I would prefer to see you become a working actor sooner rather than later, but if you have the time for a university program before starting, that is the best of all worlds. An actor who arrives on the scene having gone through, say, NYU and continued on to the Yale Drama School is going to have a much easier time of it than the equally talented actor who arrives in Hollywood with no acting training and who starts knocking on agents' doors.

Especially in the major cities, you will find many individual professional-level acting teachers. Most of them are working pros that teach. Since there is no accreditation or qualification involved to screen professional-level teachers, it is essential that you audit their classes before signing up.

Under the umbrella of private professional classes, you'll find subcategories of specialty classes for commercial audition technique, cold-reading technique, film-acting technique, and more. The best bet is always to audit if possible. These specialty classes, however, tend not to demand the kind of long-term commitment that basic acting classes do.

A Tutorial for the Aspiring Actor

I'm going to assign you a manageable background education reading list. Out of the hundreds of possible titles I could suggest, I have narrowed down the suggestions to three authors: Sharon M. Carnicke, Peter Brook, and David Mamet. My objective is to prepare you to make informed decisions when you are seeking acting training. These few books, which you should be able to read in a couple of weeks easily, will give you an overview of acting training as well as the broad currents of acting theory being taught today.

Acting training as we know it in the United States is a relatively recent historic development. Its roots spring from the work of Constantin Stanislavsky, who cofounded the Moscow Art Theatre (MAT) in 1897. It was he who developed the first systematic approach to acting training. He is the one who fathered naturalistic, psychologically based acting. If you liken the various approaches to acting theory available today to branches on a tree, the trunk of the tree is Stanislavsky's work. Virtually 100 percent of contemporary acting training defines itself in relation to Stanislavsky, either pro or con. Some teachers are inspired by the very early work he did with emotional triggers, and others are inspired by the later work he did with physical actions.

Stanislavsky's work was revolutionary in its day. He wanted actors on stage to actually experience emotion rather than pretending to do so. Before Stanislavsky, an actor's implied message to the audience was, "I'm not really feeling this way, but if I were, it would look like this." Stanislavsky, impressed by Sigmund Freud, Pavlov, and others who were pioneers in the emerging field of human psychology, figured actors ought to be able to live truthfully on stage. Ultimately, his work at the Moscow Art Theatre found its way into the United States and became the spine of Method Acting as taught by Lee Strasberg. (Yes, this is the famous Method Acting you have heard about.) Later still, Strasberg's Method broke up into various warring factions, which led to the development of the Meisner Technique, probably the most popular approach to acting today.

A clerk in New York's venerable Drama Book Shop told me that *Sanford Meisner on Acting* by Sanford Meisner and Dennis Longwell is the best-selling book on acting, aside from the various titles by Stanislavsky himself. I am not recommending Meisner's book, or those of Stanislavsky, as part of your general prep. If you want to read them later, go ahead, but for now, you are wise to stay focused on the basics, not the factions. For the record, Stanislavsky's books are *An Actor Prepares* (1936), *My Life in Art* (1952), and *Creating a Role* (1961).

Begin your study with *Stanislavsky in Focus* by Sharon Carnicke (1998). She provides the best available overview of Stanislavsky's work and painstakingly explains how Stanislavsky's theories found their way from Russia into the United States. *Stanislavsky in Focus* is a scholarly book, lavishly footnoted and referenced, which befits Sharon Carnicke's credentials as Associate Professor and Associate Dean of Theatre at the University of Southern California. She is bilingual in Russian and English and has researched original Russian source material. In my opinion, Ms. Carnicke probably knows more about Stanislavsky, his development as a teacher, and the evolution of his theories than any other theatre professional living today. She has made the man her life's work. In particular, she is to be applauded for clearing up once and for all the relationship between Lee Strasberg's Method and Stanislavsky's System.

As documented by Ms. Carnicke, Lee Strasberg wanted actors to be malleable, emotionally facile, and sensitive to direction. He wanted them to be the colors on the director's palette. This put him squarely at odds with Stanislavsky. "From the founding of the Moscow Art Theatre . . . Stanislavsky consistently demands respect for the actor as a creative artist, independent of the author who wrote the play, the designers who envision it and the director who stages it" (Carnicke 1998, 162). When actors at MAT began rehearsal for a play, the first thing Stanislavsky would have each of them do is tell the entire story of the play (163). He wanted them to be familiar with the overall story, not just with their own role.

After reading Ms. Carnicke, read Peter Brook. He has written a number of books, but the most important two are *The Empty Space* (1968) and *The Open Door* (1995). This elder statesman of the theatre is a former codirector of the Royal Shakespeare Company and currently heads the International Centre of Theatre Research, which he founded in Paris in 1971. He is my personal favorite theorist. His books are easy to read, frequently profound, always insightful. His particular gift is that he takes the long view of acting. No matter how elaborate the production or acting situation under his microscope, he insists that the transaction boil down to communication between actor and audience. After you have begun auditing acting classes and exploring the kind of acting training that is available, you will appreciate how important Mr. Brook's perspective is. It is remarkable how infrequently many acting teachers today mention the audience in their classes, let alone teach that the audience is basic to the art.

> The theatre is perhaps one of the most difficult arts, for three connections must be accomplished simultaneously and in perfect harmony: links between the actor and his inner life, his partners and the audience. (Brook 1995, 37)

Brook's books are not how-to texts. He won't tell you how to use sense memory or how to be private in public, but he will help you understand why you act, and he will continually return metaphorically to the stage as a circle drawn in the dirt. He will introduce you to the work of Antonin Artaud (*The Theatre and Its Double*), Bertolt Brecht's "alienation effect" (*Brecht on Theatre*), and the late Jerzy Growtowski

(*Towards a Poor Theatre*), with whom Brook collaborated from time to time. Artaud, Brecht, and Growtowski are three of the most important acting theorists of the twentieth century. Each of them pushes and expands the work started by Stanislavsky. To Peter Brook, Stanislavsky's theories are brilliant, but they are not the be-all and end-all of acting. They are a chapter in a larger, more inclusive assessment of the actor's art, which can be traced back thousands of years. I think Brook would understand the links between shamanism and acting.

The final book on your short reading list is *True and False: Heresy and Common Sense for the Actor* (1999) by David Mamet. Mr. Mamet is a premiere American playwright and screenwriter. He is also a curmudgeon, a rabble-rouser, and a saber rattler. You must read him with a grain of salt. In *True and False,* he goes for the jugular, dissing most American acting training as fraudulent and calling Stanislavsky a cultist and dilettante. Neither assertion is true, but that's okay. In very many ways, Mamet hits the target and, when he does, it resonates loudly. His main thesis is this: Acting training in America is of uneven quality and is chock-full of self-serving teachers and schools, people and institutions more dedicated to teaching students how to be long-term students than they are in training actors. He comes down hard on Lee Strasberg and Sanford Meisner as well—but he makes good points.

As you might suspect, *True and False* was not universally celebrated in acting and teaching circles when it was published. No matter. He's right when he's right, and someone needed to say these things. I trust that you will be an astute enough reader to discern when Mamet is being a hothead and when he is making a valid point. Anyway, if you have read the other three titles on your reading list in the order I suggest, you'll be ready to stand toe-to-toe with Mr. Mamet.

Ed Hooks' POV

The goal . . . has always been to prepare actors for
careers in professional theatre, never for work in
film or TV.

Earl Cister, Associate Dean of Yale Drama School

Writers write, and actors act. If you wanted to be a writer, you would
begin by writing, and it seems to me that if you want to be an actor,
you should begin by acting. One would not begin a creative writing
program by studying basic grammar and practicing cursive for four
months. From the start, you would read good writers and put pen to
paper. It makes no sense to me whatever for beginning actors to spend
months in "introductory" or "beginner" acting classes where they do
classroom sensory exercises and do not act. Before Stanislavsky, acting
was taught via the master/apprentice paradigm. It still works.

Acting classes in the cyber age contain a melting pot of cultures. It
is not uncommon, for example, to find a Muslim sitting next to a
Fundamentalist Christian sitting next to a Buddhist sitting next to a
Jew, all in the same class. A person's religion can come into conflict
with the demands of a scene, as for example when kissing or blasphemy is involved. Acting teachers today must be skilled at handling this
kind of conflict resolution. A student who is in conflict will frequently try to hide it from the teacher. It may escape the teacher's notice
that he is carefully avoiding scene work that involves physical intimacy or that he is literally (and cleverly) changing the text of a play,
eliminating profanity altogether or paraphrasing it. I have more than
once found myself immersed in private Socratic dialogue with a student who feels he is breaking a commitment to God by uttering an
expletive. The answer is that, surely, God must have a special love for
the person who wants to honestly explore the human condition. The
goal after all is that we all live successfully together on earth. The
beauty of drama is that we try to find the commonality among
humans. The blasphemous man and lowliest criminal are brothers to

31

the highest holy man, and we may not be able to make that point if we remove blasphemy from the script. Similarly, the primal stream of life includes lust. How can we as actors make that point if we avoid physical intimacy? There is a difference between proselytizing and acting. The actor's art demands that he confront the choir, not preach to it. It is an honorable, even courageous thing to do. The actor-as-shaman is in the same game as the religious leader. He merely comes at the task a different way.

Choosing the Right Acting Teacher

You learn how to act by doing it, not by reading books about how to do it. In this respect, learning to act is similar to learning how to ride a bicycle. By all means, read up on your subject and acquire as much background information as you can. If you are going to be riding bicycles, it's a good idea to know about air pressure in tires. If you are going to act, it's a good idea to know about Stanislavsky. Just remember that your objective is to actually get up on your feet and act, and at some point, you're going to have to put the books down and take to the stage. The selection of a good acting teacher is critical. You must trust him or her. Acting is a process of exposing yourself, not of hiding, and it is essential that you feel comfortable with your coach.

Acting teachers tend to be egoists. Every one of us thinks he is the best at what he does. Everyone believes he has figured out the most efficient route to acting magic. This fact of life complicates the new actor's quest for a teacher. Unless you have done your homework (read those books!), most every teacher you meet will know more than you do about acting. You will have no basis on which to judge anything other than a visceral emotional response to his personality and the dynamic in his classroom.

Most professional-level acting teachers will allow you to audit their class. Some of them will charge you a small fee for the privilege, but they allow it nonetheless. Occasionally, however, you will come across someone who does not allow auditors under any circumstances. (You're also unlikely to be permitted to audit university acting classes.) In such a case, you will be forced to rely on a personal interview with the teacher and the opinion of current and past students. A no-audit policy places the prospective student in a very awkward position because it is always best to take a look at a class before signing up. Remember that there is zero accreditation involved for professional acting teachers. Anybody who wants to can toss an ad in an entertainment industry trade paper and begin soliciting students. The rationale given by teachers who do not allow auditors is that their current students need to "feel safe." Outside observers will make them feel self-conscious. The teacher will tell you that he is only interested in keeping the environment private for the sake of free expression. I disagree with the reasoning and am suspicious of its effect. While a safe environment is definitely important when studying acting, it is also true that acting involves an audience. If a teacher is working so exclusively and privately on emotions and self-exploration, it may be a red flag to a prospective student.

When you audit an acting class, you sit and watch what is going on. You will see students presenting scenes and doing exercises and improvisations. Everybody in the room except you will seem to know what is going on. During break, you can chat with students, but keep in mind that they are likely to endorse the class they are paying to take.

Here are some good chatty questions you can ask students who are already in an acting class:

1. How long have you been studying with this teacher?
2. Have you studied with anybody else? What's the difference between this teacher and your former one?
3. Do you have an agent? Do you work as an actor? (If you find yourself talking to someone who has been in acting classes for four or five years and still is not working as an actor, you are talking to a professional student, not a professional actor. Keep that in mind.)

Some acting teachers may ask you to audition for their classes. This is a common situation in professional schools that have a titular head who teaches the "master" classes, while underlings teach "intro." If you are asked to audition for a class, keep in mind a point I have made repeatedly in this book, namely, that actors should lead in the performance transaction. It is easy to feel intimidated in an office audition. If you find yourself in a situation where the teacher appears to be looking down on you, or if you pick up a condescending attitude, think twice before signing up. It is quite likely that same attitude will find its way into the person's classes. It is essential that you find an acting teacher who will encourage you to work from a position of strength.

Adding to the confusion about finding a good acting teacher is the almost wholly negative influence of Hollywood on acting training. Many Hollywood acting classes are to acting training what Hollywood movies are to movies. Their agenda is too often not about art, but commerce. They are teaching what the star-struck aspiring actor is willing to buy rather than what he needs. New actors arrive by the droves in Los Angeles each year, intent on becoming movie stars, and they gravitate to acting classes that are advertised in trade papers to be movie-oriented. It's not that the training is altogether bad. The problem has more to do with the focus, the mandate of the school. If Stanislavsky were alive today and decided to open a school in Hollywood, I can't help but wonder if his primary consideration would be to build an alumni list of television actors. Somehow, I just don't think so.

Many acting teachers also capitulate to market demands by offering acting classes in which scene work is videotaped and replayed. The student is given the opportunity to be in front of a camera while he is learning how to act, which sounds like a good deal and becomes a selling point. The problem with this approach is that when a new actor is learning how to act, he really ought not to be worrying about how he is coming across on camera. Returning to the analogy about learning to act being like learning to ride a bike, you would not want a new bike rider to be thinking about how he might look in a home movie. He should be focused on riding the bike! The very last thing on a new actor's mind should be how the videotape replay will look, and he ought not to be angling himself around so the camera can see his face.

The proper sequence of training is that first you should learn the craft. Only after you have mastered the basics of playing a scene and analyzing a role should you worry about learning how to act in front of a camera. Indeed, the presence of a videotape camera in a basic acting class can be downright detrimental in my opinion. It can lead the student actor to pose for the camera, to hold positions so that the camera can see his face, to be overly concerned about facial expressions, and so on. Really, what the new actor should be thinking about is the actual playing of the scene. His attention should be on the imaginary circumstances of the scene and the reality of what his scene partner is doing, not on videotape replay or camera angles. Acting for camera as opposed to stage requires technical adjustments and an understanding of what happens in the editing room after the scenes are shot. These techniques are best learned separately rather than combined with a basic acting class. We'll talk about this more in depth in the chapter on Career Strategies.

Many new actors equate good acting with natural behavior. The thinking goes this way: "If I can speak the lines truthfully and be relaxed, I'll be a good actor." That's not enough! Theatrical reality is not the same thing as regular reality. Regular reality is what they are doing over at the 7-Eleven. Speaking truthfully is indeed a virtue, but that in itself does not give a scene theatrical value. Neither does an ability to make oneself cry on cue equate to good acting. This confusion about acting theory is understandable. If you watch a movie, it does indeed appear that the actors are simply behaving naturally and, unless you are attuned to it, you may not notice the negotiations within scenes, the conflict and obstacles that stir the characters to action. Also, many actors who are interviewed for newspaper and magazine articles wrongly explain their craft. ("The character just takes me over, that's all . . .") This is all the more reason why it is important that you, the new actor, do plenty of research before trying to select an acting class.

The Actor and the Audience

I'm having a tough time with you, Bruce, and one of the reasons is because you are audience-conscious. What makes you audience-conscious? I can understand Milton Berle being audience-conscious, but what makes you audience-conscious? Stanislavsky, no slouch, had a phrase which he called "public solitude." He said that when you're alone in your room and nobody's watching you—you're just standing in front of the mirror combing your hair—the relaxation, the complete-ness with which you do it is poetic. He calls this relaxed behavior on the stage "public solitude." On the stage public solitude is what we want. (Meisner and Longwell 1987, 43–44)

Sanford Meisner was a great man of the theatre and a master acting teacher. His past students are legion and his influence is a matter now of historical record. However, along with his invaluable contributions to acting training—the Word Repetition Game being foremost among them—he unwittingly contributed to an environment of confusion for many new actors when he spoke of the actor's relationship with the audience, as he did in the passage quoted above. Meisner's own teacher, Lee Strasberg, stepped into the same quicksand with his "private moment exercise." In their efforts to help new actors behave naturally on stage, both men encouraged at least a temporary disregard for the audience.

The basic idea behind Stanislavsky's "public solitude" is that the actor should not chase the audience with his performance. Stanislavsky got the idea from Yoga exercises that require total concentration, a sort of mental isolation (Carnicke 1998, 171). The thought was that an actor who is fully focused is inherently interesting to watch, but if that actor tried to *show* the audience what he was feeling, he would not be so interesting. As Strasberg put it, "I know many actors who develop concentration, and yet the audience never gets the sense of 'going where they are.' These actors are always coming out to join the audience. . . . One kind [of acting] comes out to you and shows and affects and demonstrates. The other kind demands that you go where it is going" (Strasberg 1965, 15–16).

Misunderstanding about "public solitude" has probably done more harm to actor training than any other single principle. It is essential that this concept be placed in a proper context, or it can lead acting students down a path of too much self-involvement. If you do not have theatrical intent, that is, an intention to communicate with the audience, acting for you may become, as Joseph Chaikin said, "a kind of flattery" (Chaikin 1972). It is understandable that a person who is encouraged to be private on stage and to exclude the audience might conclude that the most important part of acting is his own self and his own honestly expressed emotions. In that paradigm, however, the audience becomes a voyeur instead of a participant. Peter Brook enunciates the actor/audience contract correctly when he writes in *The Open Door* (1995) about the three links an actor on stage must always maintain: (1) the link between himself and his inner life, (2) the link with his scene partners, and (3) the link with the audience (37). You can't have one without the other two and, as a matter of actor training, you separate the links at your peril. Meisner, Strasberg, and Stanislavsky, with their good-intentioned efforts to help the self-conscious actor connect the link between himself and his inner life, fostered what has become a widespread misunderstanding about acting theory itself. It is essential that the cyber-age actor be clear about why he acts: for the audience, first, foremost, and exclusively. Take the audience away, even in an exercise, and you no longer have theatre. Acting is, as Sanford Meisner observed, "living truthfully under imaginary circumstances" (Silverberg 1994, 51), but the definition should be amended to include four more words: "for a theatrical purpose."

Finding Your Technique

Acting training teaches technique. The Meisner Technique is so popular these days that some actors have come to believe that there is no technique other than Meisner's, but it is not true. Technique is whatever works, and every actor develops his own. When they approach a role, some actors like to do a lot of thinking and shuffling around before they commit to a performance. Others like to make bold, strong physical commitments right from the get-go, and then change if it doesn't work. Some actors try to find the character's inner rhythms first, others ask themselves what sort of animal their character would be. Technique is a roomy umbrella, a catchall cover under which any actor can stand, regardless of his approach to a role. If you begin your exploration of a character with a consideration of his toenails, that's your business and your technique.

Whatever technique you use, it is ultimately in the service of a human-to-human theatrical transaction. We do not celebrate technique for technique's sake. (Well, maybe some people do, but they shouldn't.) Acting is an interpretative art. The actor interprets the character based on his own personal value system, presenting a performance that the audience will either relate to or not. At some point the actor is going to be alone on stage or in front of the camera with the audience. His ability to communicate is the litmus test of success as an artist.

Finally, a performance boils down to the actor's personal values, the way he comes at life. An actor is not an empty vessel. It is not our lot in life merely to express the views of the playwright and director. A person of deep religious faith will likely come up with a different interpretation of Hamlet than one who is an atheist. One actor will tend to see the pain in a character while another will tend to see the joy. It all depends on your upbringing, life influences, genetics, and education. Each actor is a product of his past and, when he acts, he puts all of that on the line. He exposes himself so that the audience may look inside itself.

"I Just Want to Act in Movies!"

A lot of new actors tell me they only want to act in movies and maybe on television. They do not want to act on stage at all. The truth is that acting is acting is acting, regardless of where you do it. In the theatre, the transaction between actor and audience is clearest. Movies and television are extensions of theatre. If you want to be a really excellent film actor, return to the basic actor-audience contract. Even if you do not aspire to a career on stage, it will benefit you to act in some stage plays. You will get immediate feedback from the audience, something that is impossible when you act in front of a camera. In the theatre, everybody is in the same room at the same time for the same reason. The members of the audience are super-responsive, like a dream lover. The Big Secret that so many new actors have not yet learned is that, when you act in front of a camera, you still must play for that audience! There is a lot of misinformation floating around about film acting. "Make it small," "be natural," "don't project," and so on. A good film actor still must be on stage, still must have a theatrical intention, still must have a strong sense of how his audience is responding. Occasionally, a movie will overtly acknowledge the audience. Woody Allen does it in his movies all the time. Charlie Chaplin played for the audience. He would look squarely into the camera lens from time to time to make sure that we knew that he knew that we were there, and that it mattered. But, for the most part, a movie audience is not confronted in this manner, and it is easy to forget it is there. This is the reason why you see so many film actors go back to do the occasional stage play. Working in the legitimate theatre is like visiting a creativity refueling station.

I know from firsthand experience what can happen when an actor gets too far removed from the actor-audience transaction. Some years ago, I had a good recurring role on a television show called *Crazy Like a Fox*. It starred Jack Warden and John Rubenstein as private eyes, and I played Pete Farmer, the forensics expert at the police lab. All of my scenes were with Jack and John. At that point in my career, I had been working steadily on television shows in Hollywood for several years. I had not been doing any plays at all, having gravitated from the world of stage in New York to the world of television in Hollywood in 1976. Well, on the day that this story takes place, I was shooting a scene on a sound stage at Twentieth-Century Fox. It was the last setup of the day, and we had already completed master shots and Jack's close-ups. The camera and crew turned their attention to me, knowing that as soon as we got this last shot, the workday would be over. I took my position, and the director called out, "Roll film!" I heard the slate click and someone in the shadows echo, "Rolling!" The director paused and then instructed, "Action!" Suddenly I entered a time warp. I felt totally, completely, overwhelmingly lost. I knew my lines, but I did not have a reason in the world to say them. There was no theatrical intention. I began to experience the worst feeling of panic you could ever imagine, and if I had not been wearing makeup, I'm sure everybody would have seen the color drain from my face. I spoke my lines on automatic pilot, calling on some deep-seated actor-survival mechanism. "Cut! Let's do it again, Ed. That was a little tight," said the director. Tight? He was lucky there was sound coming out of my mouth at all! I could see Jack Warden off to the side of the camera, giving me encouraging smiles and head nods. Being the old pro that he was, he knew something was wrong. I shot the scene again, and it must have been a bit better because this time they printed it. "That's a wrap!" called out the AD, and I headed to my dressing room, soaked with sweat and trembling.

The reason this awful experience happened to me was that I was disconnected from what actors are supposed to do. After working in Hollywood for several years, I had become accustomed to framing the shot rather than communicating the story. I knew how to work the camera for the best angle, how to hold for reaction, all that good stuff . . . and I had forgotten about the audience. I was focused on myself and a paycheck rather than on communicating with an audience.

That afternoon on the sound stage terrified me so much that I was determined that it not happen again. As soon as I figured out what had happened to me, I knew what I had to do. I went out that very week and got myself cast in a stage play, *Doctor Faustus Lights the Lights*, by Gertrude Stein. I had to get back to the audience. I had to reconnect with them. That is why I say to you: Even if your career plan is to act in movies and television, train for the stage and work on the stage. That is where the shamanistic impulse lives, and you need to stay connected with it if you want to be an excellent film actor.

Making movies isn't for everybody. Though anybody can theoretically do it, the camera favors certain personality types. Recently, I was watching the actor Harrison Ford on an interview show and was struck by his slower-than-average inner rhythms. You could not help but hang on his every word, a quality that makes him a good fit for movies. James Dean had that, too, as did Montgomery Clift and Marlon Brando in his day. Juliette Binoche is one of my personal favorite actresses these days, and she has the same quality. What I'm saying is that it is not as easy as you might think to carve out a career in movies. You can work on television shows if you're likeable, but the actor who thrives in movies has about him an air of unpredictability, even danger. The challenges you face may not be within your control. Having said that, you'll be interested in the Movies section (in the Career Strategies chapter) that deals with the digital video revolution. Digital technology is putting low-cost moviemaking power in the hands of everybody, and if you can't get cast in the big time Hollywood system, there may be other avenues for you to consider.

"*Ladies, Can We Talk?*"

I need to have a private word with the female reader of this book. You guys aren't going to like what I have to say, so go on in the other room and have a cyber cigar. I'll come and get you when we finish.

Here's the thing, ladies. As you may have figured out already, we live in a sexist and youth-obsessed society. (I could argue that ours is also a racist and oligarchic society, but that's subject matter for another conversation. For now, let's stick with the female versus male thing.) If you happen to be eighteen years old and svelte, the sexism is going to work in your short-term favor, but if you are pushing thirty and don't like to weigh yourself every day, you will have to take the bias into consideration as you make your career plans. The playing field is not level when it comes to men and women in show business. There is relatively more work for men over thirty-five than there is for women over thirty-five, even though there are more women that age than there are men in the general population.

Soapbox Fact: Sexism is more prevalent in the movie and television industry than it is in the legitimate theatre. The reason for this is that, in addition to being a sexist society, we in America are devoted to commerce. Television is about selling eyeballs to advertisers, and advertisers favor young consumers over older ones because they spend their money more freely and impulsively. "Teenagers are going to spend $160 billion this year [2000], a 60 percent increase over three years ago. That's a lot of money, and everybody wants a share" (*New York Times*, 17 September 2000). Movies—at least mainstream movies delivered up by Hollywood—are about putting butts in the seats. The big movie hits are able to deliver movie fans that will see a picture more than once. I personally know people who have seen *Star Wars* fifteen or twenty times. Again, it is the young moviegoer that will spend freely at the box office, and this is why movies target the youth market. It's all about money. This may be a frustrating situation for you, but it is what it is. Next time we get together to design a new country, we'll try to do better.

Soapbox Fact: There is nothing you can do in the short term to change existing societal prejudices. Some of us are convinced that the United States is in a period of development that is roughly analogous to the latter stages of the Roman Empire in the fourth and fifth centuries. We have a government that is run by rich, primarily white, males. Women have only a marginal elective voice in Washington, although the female vote is the most coveted by presidential candidates. The situation will improve, and the face of our government will begin to resemble the face of the American population, when enough citizens are willing to vote the status quo out of office. My advice to you is: Until the system itself changes, focus your energies on taking care of yourself within the structure as it exists. Your most powerful asset is your voice as an artist. Do not waste your valuable energies by being angry in the casting offices. Anger about the uneven playing field will only cost you income that you will need if you are to survive and contribute to changes in the status quo.

Soapbox Fact: Regarding your age, as a career strategy, it is better to position yourself on the younger end of an older type category. One of the most common errors I see women make is trying to make themselves look younger so as to fit into a younger casting call. It makes sense, because most of the work is in the younger categories, but as a strategy it is self-defeating. If you are a thirty-year-old woman who is trying to compete with twenty-year-old women, you're going to lose. Anyway, there's a quirk about advertiser psychology that is worth noting. If a casting call goes out for women in the thirty-to-thirty-five age range, you can bet your sneakers that the final casting will favor the actresses who are on the younger end of that scale. If a call goes out for women in the eighteen-to-twenty-four age range, the likelihood is that they will cast someone on the younger end of the call. This is why you are smart to stay on the younger end of an older call. This way you will move into your most comfortable age range rather than move away from it. All else being equal, the advertisers will opt for actors on the younger end of the call.

Because women in the United States are bombarded daily with hundreds, maybe thousands, of youth-oriented sales images, I understand that it may run against the grain for me to suggest that you, as a career strategy, allow yourself to age gracefully. However, that is precisely what I think you ought to do. Maintain your good health and do not buy into the rest of it. Play from a position of strength in the marketplace. By that I mean show the world who you are. Wear it on your sleeve. Do not try to be what you think they want to see because if you go that way, you'll always be one step behind the parade.

All right, thanks for listening. Somebody go tell the guys to come back in here.

The Problem with Isms

The *isms* have been one of the most positive developments of the late twentieth century. Feminism, ageism, sexism, and multiculturalism have given voice to many people who have been previously mute in our culture, a development that should be celebrated. A society that does not honor and listen to all of its members is not worth preserving. Desirable though the goal of inclusion may be, the various isms in pursuit of it can too easily harden into political correctness. When that happens, we have a problem in acting. You cannot accurately hold the mirror up to nature if you are going to exclude from view those parts that might offend somebody. We must never confuse political correctness with wisdom. As actors—shamans—we must keep asking what is true of all people. What motivates and drives us? How do we survive as a species? Why do we fight wars? What are the differences between the sexes? What is bigotry? Why is bigotry?

Do not underestimate the challenge. The isms are deeply ingrained in our daily life now and have become part of the public education that every American child receives. It is taken for granted in many quarters. More than once, I have seen actors in audition taken to task by good-intentioned, politically correct casting directors who considered the actor's monologue material to be inappropriate—either blasphemous or demeaning to women.

And it is not only in audition that the isms appear. I recall a San Francisco production of *Breaking the Code* by Hugh Whitemore that was totally ruined because the actor who portrayed Alan Turing wanted to make the character's sexual orientation a mere preference. The truth is that Turing was in the closet and in deep conflict with himself over this matter. He didn't know about gay pride and was terrified by the prospect of telling his mother the truth. The actor in that production and, presumably, his director were obviously full of goodwill and loving intentions, but they were preaching to the already converted instead of challenging the audience. What they were doing was politically correct but lacked a theatrical point.

Actors have always been citizens of the world, and this orientation is quickening noticeably in the cyber age. Communication across great distances is instantaneous now, and international travel is commonplace. The world we have grown up with is reorganizing into communities of ideas rather than geographically separate nation-states.

The shifting tide of international values was brought home to me in a *New York Times* piece by Suzanne Daley (9 April 2000) who posted from Paris. She pointed to the widening chasm between traditional European cultures and the United States. Since the fall of communism, the United States has become like an eight-hundred-pound gorilla to many Europeans, perceived as tramping around the globe demanding that things be done the American way. There is a new arrogance in how the U.S. government deals with other countries, knowing that there is not a chance that an unhappy government might toss its lot in with Russia. The United States is thought to be shouting, like *Titanic* director James Cameron at the Oscars, "I'm king of the world!" This is furthering international divisions along philosophical lines.

Ms. Daley, in her article, enumerated these glaring disparities between European and U.S. cultures:

1. A record number of Americans now own firearms while, in Europe, personal firearms are shunned.
2. Thirty-eight U.S. states now enforce the death penalty while the sentence has been abolished or suspended by every member of the European Union.
3. Forty-eight percent of Americans do not have health insurance; large American cities are plagued with homelessness. Cradle-to-grave health care is a birthright in Europe.
4. The U.S. "war on drugs," which treats drug abuse as a crime instead of a public health problem, is in stark contrast to drug policies in Europe.
5. The United States is essentially incarcerating its lower classes, spending more on prisons now than on education. Half of the prisoners in the federal jails are there for violating drug laws.
6. Black youths in America are more than six times as likely as whites to be sentenced to prison by juvenile courts. For drug offenses, blacks are sent to prison forty-eight times more often than whites charged with the same crimes.

Acting is about basic human values, what it means to live successfully in the world. Just as a religious leader like the Pope seeks the underlying values in all of the world's societies, so too must the actor. Even if we are acting on a television situation comedy, we still traffic in matters spiritual. The actor needs to ask the hard questions. Does successful living equate to stock options and a hot IPO? A new car? A meaningful relationship? Freedom from censorship? Does successful living equate to freedom from government intervention in our lives, even if that freedom includes zero health care?

The point is frequently made that our very fragile legitimate theatre culture will ultimately survive in an electronic age precisely because it is small. There will always be, so goes the thinking, a dozen or so people who will get together for a good play, even if they have to do it in the library basement. That is probably true, but it seems to me that this is not the evolution on which we actors should be pinning our hopes. We are looking now at a global audience, something that has not even existed until recently. We have a fresh pony to ride. We should be expanding our reach internationally as artists in the cyber age.

It is easy for us to look no further than our immediate environment, and tempting to conclude that American values are celebrated by the whole world, but it's not so. Any American who travels internationally will immediately see that there are other perspectives in the world. Speaking just for myself—and totally unscientifically—I have noticed that citizens in Europe do not so quickly ask what I do for a living. In the United States, the subject of professions comes up quickly in almost any casual conversation because, in America, our worth is associated with our jobs and earning power. It seems to me that in Europe, the prevailing idea is that people have intrinsic value that supercedes a paycheck. We as artists have a moral and shamanistic obligation to stay connected with the stream of core human values, not just the values of the prevailing U.S. culture.

Finding the Survival Mechanism

In the pages that follow, I am going to lay out my own personal perspective on the values behind acting. I do it not to preach or infuse, but to stimulate you to think about such things and to develop your own perspectives. Many novice actors erroneously believe that the main challenge in acting is learning all those lines and speaking them truthfully. That is like saying that the main challenge in painting is dipping a brush in paint and putting it on canvas. Learning and speaking lines is not nearly as difficult as most nonactors think it is, and acting is about much more than that. The actor speaks to the audience about life on this earth and how we survive as individuals and as a species. Words are only one tool.

All animal species on earth, including humans, act to survive. Nature has wired us that way. If we do not survive and create the next generation, our species dies out. The difference between us humans and lower forms of animals is that we have a brain that gives us the option of making choices in life that are counter to our best interests. Bears and elephants and monkeys operate on instinct and have no real choice about their behavior. Humans, for example, can know that something—like smoking, for instance—is bad for their health and still do it anyway. Lower animals can be forcefully addicted to something like nicotine in a laboratory setting, but, left to their own instincts, would never inhale cigarette smoke a second time if given the option. The wondrous distinction of humans is our ability to think, to choose our paths in life, to err and to succeed, and to experience complex emotions. Unlike other animals, we have the potential to experience exhilarating happiness and mind-numbing pain. On that platform rests all of the arts.

We all act to survive whether we are living in a primitive society where fire is made by rubbing sticks together or whether we live in a complex metropolis like New York City or Tokyo. Regardless of how or where we do it, we all must eat, and we all must sleep, and we have to find ways to get along with one another. Think about this: When a baby is born, the first thing it does is try to live; when a person is dying, the last thing he does is try to live. In between birth and death, we make choices and take actions every day that we think best serve our survival. Clearly, we do not always make the best choices, and some of us go totally off the civilized track. Adolf Hitler wrongly thought he was making the best survival choices. A person who robs a bank or begins shooting an assault weapon in an office building is making a very bad choice but, at that moment, he will contend that violence is his best possible option. Courtrooms all over the world are continually processing people who have made bad choices in life. Many of them are deemed to be insane, mentally ill, or incompetent and are hospitalized. Some are adjudged to be sane but misguided and wrongheaded, and we put them in jails and prisons, or we execute them. These are extreme cases, however, judged against a general standard of right and wrong. The family of humans is a big one, containing extremes of all kinds, but most of us live lives in which we do no harm to others and in which we simply try our best to thrive. We fall in love, work jobs, have children, go to church or temple, treat our sicknesses, take vacations, listen to music, fight wars, read books, laugh, and cry. We negotiate status with one another and we jockey for position at the front of as many lines in life as possible. We make messes of our affairs and relationships because we are neither infallible nor omniscient, and we clean them up the best way we know how. We neither rob banks nor own AK-47s, and we do not know how to construct bombs. Most of us ride in the main current of the broad river we call humanity. These are the things that define us, and they are the subject matter of all art, including the actor's art. Drama since ancient Greece has focused not on man's relationship with God, but with man's relationship with man.

Now, given this platform and context, consider once again the actor as shaman. I contend it is our job as actors to think about things like survival, birth, and death and to report what we discover to the tribe. It is our job not to judge our fellow humans but to understand them. It is our mandate to help the tribe understand itself, to illustrate how it is that we humans are all part of the same big family and are all motivated by the same pursuit of successful survival. It is a powerful thing to be an actor, an honorable calling. Most people in the world do not confront the essential elements of humanity in this kind of conceptual way. It is the realm of philosophers, poets, and artists. This is why I say that acting is—or should be—so much more than simply heading for Hollywood to be a movie star. Actors are important to society, and I believe this will become increasingly obvious in the cyber age.

Using Primal Analysis

In my acting classes, I encourage a "primal analysis" of scenes. It is based on evolutionary psychology and the self-evident premise that all of us, including the characters we portray, act to survive. We *need* to survive, are *driven* to survive. If an actor can tap into the primal stream of a character, it can make for extraordinarily powerful theatre. What is the underlying current that is driving the character? Why, for instance, does Lady Macbeth prod her husband to commit murder? How will murder be in her perceived self-interest? The answer is that it will speed her husband's ascension to the throne, and it is in her primal self-interest to be married to a king rather than a subject. She experiences this as a need and not merely a want or simple preference. She doesn't say to herself, "It would be nice to be married to a king but, hey, if it doesn't work out, I'll take in washing to help make ends meet." No, she is driven to manipulate her husband into murder, risking her own life and his if the plot is discovered, because Macbeth is not the kind of man who would do it on his own. Can you see how this makes for compelling acting? You have to motivate Lady Macbeth somehow, right? One way or the other, the words are going to come out of the actor's mouth. How do you justify her actions? Do you write her off as a lunatic that is hell-bent on murder, a fringe character in dramatic history? No! If you do that, you put her on the same ash heap as Hitler and other fringe characters. Great theatre emerges when the actor shows the audience how this character is like itself. It is the actor's job to create in the audience a sense of empathy with the character she is playing. It does this great character of Lady Macbeth a disservice to render her merely demented and obsessed. She is worth more than that. She *must* arrange for Duncan's murder! Like all of us, she is driven to survive. In her case, the drive results in murder. In us all, there is the potential for murder. If the actor can help us see that, then her performance has risen to the level of art and not mere entertainment.

Here is another example of a primal analysis: You have been cast to portray Keely in *Keely and Du* by Jane Martin. She is a character that becomes pregnant and, when she goes to a clinic to get an abortion, is kidnapped by members of an antiabortion group. Their goal is to keep her restrained until she is too far into her pregnancy for abortion, thereby saving her baby's life and making a point. The play's central story revolves around the relationship formed between Keely and the older antichoice woman who is her jailer. Now, on the surface of it, the arc of Keely's character is pretty straightforward. She wants an abortion, is thwarted, and must overcome the obstacle of captivity in order to terminate her pregnancy. As written, the character expresses no second thoughts or regrets about abortion. The play's author focuses the spotlight on the issue of freedom of choice and women's rights. But what would happen to the acting if Keely were in conflict with herself about the procedure of abortion? A primal analysis would suggest that nature is driving Keely to go full term and deliver the baby. She may choose to abort, and we may argue about whether she should have the choice, but what does nature say about it? From nature's perspective, a medical abortion is not a natural thing. It is an interventionist procedure. If the actress portraying Keely can get in touch with this internal drive, then she will have to do much more to override the primal stream with her thinking brain. In other words, a primal analysis opens the possibility of yet more conflict for the actor, and conflict is always a fruitful thing. It puts Keely's head into conflict with her heart. It doesn't matter that there are no words in the script that overtly state Keely's conflict about abortion. It doesn't matter that all of the antiabortion rhetoric comes from Du's mouth. A primal analysis will cause Keely to react differently to Du than she would if there were no conflict within her about the abortion. A primal analysis will enrich the characterization.

Consider the David Mamet play *Glengarry Glen Ross*, set in a Florida real estate office. The salesmen employed there are hustlers who are bent on accumulating commissions even if the land they are selling is worthless. How do you approach these kinds of roles? Where are the characters' ethics? How can they sleep comfortably at night after ripping off unsuspecting people all day long? Most of us would say, "Hey, I would never do that kind of thing for a living. It's dishonest. I'd feel bad about myself." A primal analysis, however, would justify the behavior. From the perspective of one of the salesmen, the higher value is the accumulation of money. A man does what a man must do in order to get his share of the pie in a world that is corrupt at the core anyway. Eat or be eaten; life is war, and only the strongest survive; each day at the office is like a day on the battlefield; it is not necessary to know your enemy, only to defeat him. In other words, from a primal perspective, a man has no option in life except to fight for his survival. He is driven to do whatever he has to—in this case, it's shilling worthless real estate. He must sell it; he needs to sell it; it's in his self-interest to sell it. We who are sitting in the audience can

49

recognize the battlefield ambiance of the business office. We can relate to the behavior of the characters in a primal way, even if we are personally not selling worthless goods.

In *The Days of Wine and Roses* by J. P. Miller, Joe and Kristen are husband-and-wife alcoholics. Their lives have been ruined by alcohol, and the defining event in the play is when Joe joins Alcoholics Anonymous. The actors that play these roles must justify alcoholism. The easy choice is to write it off as a genetic predisposition, something that runs in the family. Though there may be truth in that analysis, it isn't helpful theatrically. From an acting perspective, it is better to put the choice to drink within the character's control. A primal analysis would ask the question: "How does drinking serve this character's perceived self-interest?" Why does this person need to see the world through inebriated eyes? Could it be that the effects of alcohol protect the character from having to confront the harshness and competitiveness of life? Could it be that, from the character's perspective, the act of living is too painful to bear? If life is painful, and if you are being driven to survive, then you might get drunk in order not to feel the pain. If you do not feel the pain, you prolong your life. We in the audience are going to have a peak theatrical experience if we can recognize in ourselves the imperative to mask pain. It will not be as satisfying if the character on stage is an alcoholic if we in the audience are not. We will merely look at such a person and say, "Well, thank goodness I don't have that problem!" No! The art lies in the actor's ability to show us in the audience how we are family to the character on stage, how we share his drives. We do not all become alcoholics, but we do all act to survive. That is the point of empathy.

Another cornerstone of the primal analysis is that females have different survival and mating strategies than men. Women are not men in skirts. They have a different biology altogether. For starters, a man can reproduce hundreds of times a year if he can convince enough women to cooperate with him, and he can do this all the way into his old age. A woman, by contrast, can only reproduce once per year, and nature slams the lid on her ability to reproduce at all beyond a certain midlife point. Because reproducing is a relatively bigger deal for a woman than it is for a man, she has an incentive to mate with someone who will make a significant investment in the relationship. She has a limited number of opportunities to successfully pass on her genes to the next generation, and she needs to get the odds working in her favor. She needs to find a man who is not only genetically attractive (broad chest, bright eyes, and so on) but also likely to stick around long enough to support and protect their offspring to the point where the children can survive on their own.

The male generally resists a long-term commitment to a single woman because he has so much more potential to reproduce. This is why men tend to be more sexually aggressive than women and why women tend to be choosier about whom they mate with than men do. It is in the male's genetic best interest to father children with many women, and it is in the female's genetic best interest to draw a commitment from a single good-candidate male. These conflicting strategies are the source of sexual tensions going all the way back to Adam and Eve, and they are the stuff of great drama. It may not be politically correct, but acting is no place for political correctness in the first place.

Seen though an evolutionary prism, life is a big mating dance, with everybody choosing mates and having children the best way they know how. This is not to say that humans are conceptual about their sexual choices. On the contrary, we operate most always on emotion. "Understanding the often unconscious nature of genetic control is the first step toward understanding that—in many realms, not just sex—we're all puppets, and our best hope for even partial liberation is to try to decipher the logic of the puppeteer" (Wright 1994, 37).

Nature has done a lot of our prethinking for us, leaving us wired us to feel good about the things that are good for our continuation as a species, and to be repulsed by the things that are bad for us. Infanticide repulses; falling in love feels good. Suicide is sadly confusing; protecting one's child from harm feels good. The reason the story of Medea has struck a responsive chord for so many thousands of years is that infanticide is particularly repulsive emotionally. Women are not supposed to murder their babies, right? Nature has wired us that way.

Remember the Susan Smith case? A young South Carolina mother strapped her two young sons into their car seats and sent the car into a lake, drowning them. The prosecution for that case argued that she did her horrible deed because her children were an obstacle to a budding romance with the town's most eligible bachelor. The District

Attorney contended that Susan's boyfriend did not want children, and so she murdered them. I never bought that explanation. To me, it was a Medea situation. For a period of time after Susan Smith's conviction, I collaborated on the writing of a stage play inspired by the case, and I had the opportunity to investigate it more deeply than the casual observer. Though I doubt she was conceptual about it, I am convinced Ms. Smith killed those kids as an act of vengeance against her husband, a man who had been unfaithful to her and had abandoned her. It's Darwinian. She chose a man with whom to mate and, when their second child was still in diapers, he was out the door. She, an hourly wage-earner in a grocery store, was left to raise the babies alone, and it infuriated her. If you kill a man, you kill him once. If you kill a man's children, you kill him again and again and again. Susan Smith was at the time of the killings young enough to bear more children, with another yet-to-be-found husband who would hopefully not desert her. Postscript: As this book was being prepared for printing, it came to light that Susan Smith, incarcerated at the Women's Correctional Institution in Columbia, South Carolina, for the next fifty years, has been having sexual relations with a prison guard. News reports are that she is pregnant. This also make primal sense. The field of prospective mates for the woman has shrunk to the occupants of a single state prison. She chose from among them. If an actress were portraying Susan Smith in a movie, the strong primal choice would be to follow her need to procreate.

Othello killed Desdemona because he thought she was being unfaithful to him. In a primal analysis, this makes sense because the thing that will most quickly send a male into a rage is the idea that his mate is sleeping with another male. Males have a genetic incentive to make certain they are raising their own offspring, not those of some other man. Othello had incorrect information and was misinformed by Iago, but Shakespeare got it right from a Darwinian perspective. Nature would indeed wire Othello to be furious if he believed Desdemona was unfaithful.

Recently I watched two of my acting students perform a scene in which the female character makes a straightforward sexual play for the other character, a married man. I asked the actor why she was doing that, and she explained that she liked sex. I suggested a primal analysis. The key is in figuring out what the character wants from the married man. If it is merely sex, we don't have much of a scene. We only have a roll in the hay, and the average person doesn't want to pay the price of admission just to see that. If, however, she wants him to leave his wife and marry her, then we have a more powerful scene, one that makes primal sense and speaks to the human drama. It doesn't matter that there is no dialogue that spells out this objective for the woman. She's coming on sexually, and that's enough. Maybe the character herself isn't even conscious of why she's doing it. Maybe the *playwright* was not conceptual about it! As I say, nature has done a lot of pre-thinking for us. When the actress took this note and applied it, her sexual approach to the man took on an air of more significance, and it made for a better scene. Primal analysis works.

The Audience

Finding Points of Empathy

Audiences empathize with emotion, not facts. You could even say that they put up with information in order to get to the emotion. That is why Antonin Artaud said that actors are athletes of the heart. In life, we humans relate to one another emotionally. When your best friend announces that she is getting married, it makes you happy because she is happy. It is the emotion that is important, not the act of marriage itself, which is just a bunch of words and flowers. When you are having dinner with friends and someone accidentally cuts his finger while dicing the carrots, you flinch in an empathic response. It not the metal blade, sharp edge, or bread that makes you flinch. It is that you too have cut yourself at times, and you know how it feels. You relate to your friend's emotions. It is a matter of empathy.

The word *empathy* was coined by Theodore Lipps in 1907. Translated from the German *Einfühlung*, it literally means "feeling into." This is different from *sympathy*, which means "feeling for." You can feel sorry for someone and not empathize with him. Brechtian theatre excepted, the actor's primary job is to create in the audience a sense of empathy. You must get the person in the audience to identify with—to empathize with—the character you are playing. Acting rises above simple entertainment and becomes art only when the person in the audience can identify in himself the potential to behave as the character you are portraying behaves. The fact that Brutus betrays Caesar is interesting, but the thing that makes it drama is how Brutus feels about having betrayed the man.

A mother will empathize with the feelings of her baby. A lover will empathize with the sexual joy of her partner. A hustler empathizes with the feelings of his mark. When you select a birthday present for your friend, you empathize with the feelings he will likely have when he unwraps it. Nothing is more fundamental to the actor's art than a search for empathy, so let's push the microscope in for an even closer look. Let's deconstruct the matter a bit further. If we humans empathize with emotion, then what exactly *is* emotion? What is the definition of an emotion? Is it a feeling? If so, then what is a feeling? Do emotions just sort of hover around a person, striking at random? Is there a cause and effect? Do hormones cause emotions?

The best definition of an emotion that I have found is this: An emotion is an automatic value response. An emotion will automatically happen. It is a result of thinking and genetic predisposition. Your emotional reaction to a given event will be different from mine because we have different values. Example: Let's say you are walking to your car in a darkened parking lot after a late-night business meeting. Nobody else is there. As you are fifty yards from your car, you hear sounds behind you. Mentally, you identify the sounds as footsteps. As soon as you do that, the automatic value response starts. If you have been previously robbed or injured in a dark place, your automatic value response will be one of alarm. If, on the other hand, you have been living in a country like China or Singapore, where street crime is almost nonexistent, you might have quite a different automatic value response. You see what I mean? Walking, sidewalk, footsteps—those are just things, shoe leather on concrete. Nothing much matters about any of that until emotion—value judgment—enters the equation. The next time you watch a scary movie, pay attention to your own reactions. You can see the axe-wielding intruder creeping into the living room, and you are afraid . . . for the hero! You are empathizing with how she is going to feel when she sees the man.

Playing Victims

There is a difference between being a victim and being victimized. The audience will empathize with the person that is victimized and is trying to survive. It will distance itself from a person who plays the part of the victim.

Have you ever had a friend that complains all the time? She complains about her life and the trouble she has with men. She complains about her aching back, her empty bank account, and her lack of options. You, being the good friend that you are, lend an attentive and supportive ear . . . for a while. At a certain point, you will begin to say to yourself, "Hey, it's time for her to get her stuff together. We all have problems. That's life." If your friend continues to pity herself, you will begin to back off. You care about her, but you know that if you were in her position, you would pull yourself up by your bootstraps and move on with life. Audiences are like that, too. Drama is about how we humans survive in the world. Nobody goes to the theatre to learn how people give up. In other words, we are wired by nature to recognize and support the survival mechanisms in one another. A person who is full of self-pity, who is an eternal victim, is going in the wrong direction. As an acting choice, self-pity is deadly. It may be understandable behavior on a short-term basis, but as a policy in life, it becomes unpleasant. Your audience will shift from empathy into sympathy.

Emotion Leading to Action

Thinking tends to lead to conclusions; conclusions lead to emotions; emotion tends to lead to action. When you hear the footsteps behind you on the dark street, you have an emotional response. Based on the emotional response, you tend to take an action. You may quicken your pace, turn around to see who is behind you, reach into your purse, and grasp the can of pepper spray. First come the thoughts, the recognition of the facts. Then comes the emotion. Then comes the action.

A person has a fear of flying. This fear is a value response. Thinking is what led her to consider flying to be dangerous in the first place. Her emotion (automatic value response) causes her to do something about it. She may cling tightly to the armrests of her seat or breathe deeply to prevent fainting or count backward from five so as to take her mind off the fear. Emotion tends to lead to action.

It is true that the way you feel will tend to make you behave in certain ways. This is, as we have discussed, the reality that supports Strasberg's Method. Emotion tends to lead to action. It is, however, also true that this can work in reverse. The way you behave will tend to make you feel a certain way. A strategy that a psychologist might use with a troubled patient is to ask him how it might feel if his troubles vanished magically. "Suppose you were no longer afraid of flying? How would that feel?" He will then try to get the patient to behave as if that were true, as if the trouble was gone. Amazingly, if you behave as if the trouble is gone, you begin to *feel* like the trouble is gone! This is the reality that supports Stanislavsky's Method of Physical Action. Emotion and action are a two-way street.

For proof of this very valuable acting lesson, wait until the next time you are having a really down day. Wait until you are feeling lousy and depressed. Then go into the bathroom, look at yourself in the mirror and force a laugh. Even though the last thing you want to do is laugh, go ahead and do it. You will immediately feel a lightening of your emotions. Paul Ekman, a psychology professor at the University of California San Francisco, along with Wallace Friesen and Robert Levenson, conducted some fascinating experiments with professional actors in 1983 (Ekman, Levenson, and Friesen 1983). They instructed the actors to move and pose specifically selected facial muscles while simultaneously measuring such factors as heart rate, forearm muscle tension, temperature, and skin resistance. What they found out is that when a person mechanically makes a facial expression, his body will react. It is precisely what Stanislavsky would have predicted.

Crying

Crying is a fundamental human behavior—liquid emotion. "Weeping is exclusively human. As far as we know, no other animal produces emotional tears. Some people have claimed that elephants cry, weeping at being reunited with their handlers, for instance, or after being scolded. But no independent confirmation of these rare and anomalous tears has ever been made" (Lutz 1999, 17). We immediately empathize with another person's tears. Correction: We immediately empathize with a person's *honest* tears. Many weak actors are able to make themselves cry on cue. The trick to crying is to remember that usually people in life try not to cry. An actor who cries too easily makes the audience suspicious. Keep in mind that the tears are a result of something, not a cause. Find the survival mechanism. Let the tears take care of themselves.

I asked a psychiatrist once why it is that people cry at weddings if the occasions are so happy. Aren't tears an expression of sadness? He explained that we empathize with the feelings of the newlyweds and that a wedding includes both joy and pain. Yes, the couple is looking forward to a happy life together, but they are simultaneously losing their childhood and carefree ways. A wedding is a moment of symbolic passage into adulthood and responsibility. The participants may soon have a family of their own. In short, it is time to get serious about life. We who are sitting in the pews watching the wedding experience complex emotional responses because we have already endured some of life's bumps and potholes. We know what it means to give up the innocence of youth. No longer will the groom run through the living room calling out, "Hey, Dad, let me have the car!" Now he will have to earn his own money and buy his own car and worry about lending it to his own kid. No longer will the bride talk on the phone in her bedroom late into the night. Happy moments and sad at the same time. Memories and prospects, gain and loss. We cry about those things.

Heroes and Villains

A villain is a regular person that has a fatal flaw. Suppose you are hired to portray an evil person, a serial killer, let's say. The uninventive acting choice is to figuratively twirl your moustache and smirk as you kick the dog down the stairs. The audience will boo and hiss and agree with you that this character is truly nasty. The more interesting choice—and the one more likely to create a sense of empathy in the audience—would be to find the survival mechanism in the killer. What is it that draws him to his victims? Is he a man who feels powerless in life? Does he need to control people in order to feel powerful? A serial killer may be full of self-loathing but, at some level, he is making what he considers to be the best choices available to him. Neither you nor I would make those choices, but as an actor, we have to find in ourselves the *potential* to make those choices. A talented actor will not simply illustrate the fact that the character is a killer; he will find in himself the impulse and imperative to kill and hold up to view the mechanism so the audience can see it. Why *must* the character kill?

One of the defining characteristics of a sociopath is that he lacks the ability to feel empathy. If he empathized with the feelings of his victims, he would not harm them in the first place. I remember a murder case in California in which the killer broke into a home in the early evening, slaughtered an entire family, and then sat down at their dinner table and calmly ate his fill of their unfinished dinner meal. There would be no way to portray such a character in a movie other than to remove the ability to empathize from him.

A hero is a regular person who gets swept up in an extraordinary situation and must prevail. Cary Grant gets on the subway for a routine trip uptown and the next thing he knows, he's chasing the bad guys across the face of Mount Rushmore (*North by Northwest*). Gary Cooper is going about the routine business of keeping peace in his sleepy western town when word comes that a criminal he helped convict has been released from prison and is coming for revenge (*High Noon*). A woman who works at a nuclear plant becomes a whistleblower when she discovers potentially deadly breaches in safety standards (*Silkwood*).

Cyber Intermission (Watch a Charlie Chaplin Movie)

I'll admit it. I'm a knock-kneed fan of Charlie Chaplin. The man was a certifiable genius, whose particular contribution was his bringing empathy to film comedy. For that reason alone, every student actor ought to pop some corn and study the man's work. But more important, if you can act in comedy, there is a greater likelihood that you will be paid to act. Television is about commercials, and both the programs and the spots themselves tend to be lighthearted. Some actors are terrified of comedy, considering themselves to be more serious souls. For those people, Chaplin movies can be a major revelation. Watch Chaplin's movies as if they were made last year instead of seventy years ago. Remember, in his day, there were no performing unions, and so he was able to spend weeks on a single shot. Despite the apparent effortlessness of his work, whatever you see in a Chaplin movie was done on purpose.

Before Chaplin, film comedy consisted of pratfalls à la the Keystone Kops. A person would slip on a banana peel and fall on his bottom, and it was supposed to be a laugh riot. Chaplin came along and stepped on the same banana peel—and was embarrassed by it! He looked around to see if anybody noticed he had done a foolish thing. Chaplin understood that the comedy was not in the falling, but in the feelings of the fall-ee.

Another of Chaplin's remarkable insights was that comedy is drama enhanced, enlarged, raised to a higher level. He understood that underneath good comedy is a scene that will play seriously. He consistently searched for the underlying human truth in his comedy rather than hitting the laughs with a rubber mallet. In this regard—and I realize I say this at the risk of starting open warfare—Chaplin had it all over Buster Keaton. Keaton was a marvelous clown, but he consistently went for the gags rather than the humanity. He sought sympathy with his laughs rather than empathy.

In particular, I recommend that you watch *Gold Rush*, *City Lights*, and *Modern Times*. Observe how Chaplin walks a fine line between tragedy and comedy, how he pulls your heart one minute and kicks you in the rear the next. Watch his movies more than once. The first time, give in to the sheer entertainment of them. The second time, deconstruct the craft of one of the towering theatrical geniuses of the twentieth century. There is much to be learned from Charlie Chaplin that can be carried forward into the cyber future.

Bertolt Brecht

Bertolt Brecht was a famous director and playwright, the author of classics such as *The Caucasian Chalk Circle*, *Baal*, *Mother Courage*, and *The Resistible Rise of Arturo Ui*. I am bringing him up right now because he specifically aspired to a state of nonempathy in his plays. You might consider him the anti-Stanislavsky. He wanted the audience never to forget it was an audience, never to "get lost" in the action and emotion of the play. He considered theatre to be basically political. Brecht figured that the theatre should help people learn how to master life. How could they learn how to master life if they were themselves being mastered and manipulated by the actors on stage? He wanted the audience to remain alienated from the action, to always be aware of the distance between an actor and his character. Like Stanislavsky, he wanted his actors to experience emotion, but he never wanted the audience to forget or become unaware that the stimulation of emotion was a theatrical trick.

Unless you are in a Brechtian production, none of this will matter much. You ought to know about it as part of your overall theatrical training, but virtually all of the acting you will do in your career, whether it is in movies or television or on stage, will hinge on your ability to generate in the audience a sense of empathy.

Career Strategies

Seeking Representation

In order to get auditions for worthwhile roles in paying projects, you will need to be represented by an effective, enthusiastic, well-connected talent agent. The pursuit of such representation is a major activity for actors, so it will help you to know how the game of representation is played in New York and Los Angeles.

Think of the world of talent agencies as a pyramid. At the top of the pyramid are a few agencies that traffic mainly in percentage-of-gross performers and package deals. The venerable William Morris Agency is a good example, frequently representing not only the stars of a movie or TV show but also packaging its producer and writer. Slightly below the top are those who represent and cast the strong supporting roles and series regulars and, in yet another subsection, there are the agents and casting directors who spend their time brokering costar and guest star actors. Near the base of the pyramid, we find those who cast and represent the under-fives and the day-players. They tend to work on roles that are named for function rather than character: Waitress Number One, Big Cop, Delivery Boy, Street Person. Extra players do not appear on the pyramid at all and are generally considered by the talent brokers to be nonactors, human furniture.

It would be nice if you could land an agent at the top of the pyramid when you first arrive in Hollywood, but the chance of that happening is practically zero. The brokers at that level will meet you only if you have major stage credits, serious acting training, or some other kind of entree. Graduates of the Yale School of Drama, the NYU Tisch School of Drama, and Juilliard School of Drama, for example, will always receive a cursory glance from top agents just to see if there is a new Meryl Streep or Robin Williams among them. If an actor received rave reviews in a Broadway play last season, he will get meetings with the Big Boys.

At least once a month, I counsel—frequently via e-mail—a new actor who is trying to decide whether to move to L.A. or New York.

Most of the time, I take her age into account. If she is still in her teens, I urge her to get a university education before committing to either coast. The ideal is a strong liberal arts education combined with training in a dynamic drama program. If she is in her midtwenties, I try to determine if she is hell-bent on stardom, or if she actually wants to be an actor. If she tells me straightforward that she wants to be in movies and television shows, I generally suggest she head for L.A. right away. She might as well. The older she is, the less currency she will have in Hollywood. On the other hand, if it seems that she really wants to be an actor, I generally recommend New York. There she can study and develop confidence by working in the theatre, off Broadway, and off-off Broadway. If she goes to Hollywood, she'll start right away chasing the casting directors and agents. In Marlon Brando's day, New York was the center for art *and* commerce for actors, but no more. Though New York is certainly not a pristine sanctuary for the arts by any means, most raw commerce has migrated to the West Coast. If you want to seek representation and start pursuing income from acting right away, L.A. is the better destination.

I have already written a book that goes into deep detail about talent agents and how to get them, and there is not much sense in my repeating myself here. For now, just make note that you need an agent and, if you do not know how to get one, pick up a copy of my other book. It is entitled *The Audition Book: Winning Strategies for Breaking into Theatre, Film, and TV* (2000b) and is available in a revised third edition, published by Backstage Books. The book is a soup-to-nuts guide to the business of acting as well as a primer on audition technique for commercials, stage, movies, and television shows. Please visit my website at <http://www.edhooks.com> for a full review plus links to places where you can buy it.

Self-Fulfilling Prophesies

Put yourself for a moment in the position of a director that is casting a movie. You're sitting in a small office in a building on the Paramount lot in Hollywood. It's late afternoon, and the air-conditioning protects you from the heat outside. The casting director ushers in the next actor, a pleasant-looking young man with a sweaty handshake and tight smile. Before the actor has even read a single line of the script, you already know you don't want to cast him. It's not that he is physically wrong for the role, and it's not that he has a weak resume. It's also not that he can't act. Yet, you have made up your mind. He hasn't even sat down, and you're ready to thank this fellow for coming and move on to the next actor. What's going on? How can you make such a strongly negative judgment when all the fellow has done is enter the room?

Now put yourself in the shoes of that sweaty-handed actor. It probably started before you even left home. In the first place you are unemployed. Nothing unusual about that, since 85 percent of all actors are unemployed at any given moment. On the way to Paramount, you had plenty of time to think about how much you need this gig, which made you feel even worse. You arrived at the studio and discovered nobody left a drive-on pass for you at the gate, so you had to park your car four blocks away and walk back in the hot sun. You finally arrived, sweating, at the waiting room and took your seat among the other actors, each of whom seems to be more confident about things than you are. By the time the casting director cheerfully escorts you into the audition room, you already know in your heart that this job is not going to be yours.

The transaction between you and the director is complex. He needs to get his project cast, and you need a job, a trade-off that seems straightforward enough. But before you can begin to transact on that matter, you have to get the status negotiation working right. The reason the director turned off the moment you stepped into the room is that you projected a low-status, self-doubt dynamic.

Let's go back to basics. The actor leads and the audience follows. That's the natural order of things; it's been that way ever since actors were shamans and the stage was a circle in the dirt. Do you figure those ancient shamans got stage fright? You think they worried about their ability to lead? No, they didn't, and I'll tell you why. It is because they knew they were valuable. They knew they were important to the tribe. When you walk into that office on the Paramount lot, nobody cares. You are on your own, alone with your dreams, ambition, fear, and trepidation. The working environment for the twenty-first-century actor is harsh. It is easy to feel insignificant and unimportant at an audition.

You arrive to join a room full of nervous actors waiting to go into the audition room and, when you get inside, there are those strangers behind the table who are rendering judgments about your worthiness. It's a tough and intimidating situation, no question about it. The good news is that you don't have to feel that way. Just remember these two points:

□ Act as though you have been chosen, and you will begin to feel as if you have been chosen. Success and failure are self-fulfilling prophesies.

□ Every time you enter an audition room or walk onto a sound stage to shoot a scene, you start a status transaction. The actor leads and the audience follows.

Commercials

Your career strategy should include acting in commercials if you care about making money. Advertisers spend upward of $20 billion per year on television commercials. Members of the Screen Actors Guild currently earn about $700 million each year from them, almost as much as is earned from television shows and movies combined. And regardless of how the ultimate balance of power shifts between network television, cable networks, and the Internet, advertising is here to stay. We are, after all, living in the United States, a country that worships at the altar of consumerism. Advertising is our middle name, and commercials are the heartbeat of our economic system.

Let's be clear about something up front. You do not need to be an actor to do commercials any more. Over half of all commercials produced today do not have any words for the actors to say. If you possess a nonthreatening sense of life, are a happy camper, and want to chase after the work, then you too can do commercials. It hasn't always been this way. When I shot my first commercial in 1970 (for Holiday Inn), virtually all commercials were sixty seconds long and had wall-to-wall copy. They consisted of talk, talk, talk, and more talk. Nonactors were locked out of the process because they had to compete with well-trained actors and would fall apart when confronted with the necessity to memorize copy.

MTV and the arrival of the television remote-control device changed everything almost overnight. Advertisers began producing commercials that were visually arresting, even mesmerizing to the viewer. The goal became to keep the channel surfer from clicking away during commercial breaks, and advertisers figured out that they could not assure this behavior with words alone. The most potent commercials nowadays boil down to visual images and high-impact emotional snapshots.

In order to get commercial auditions, you will need to be represented by one or more talent agents in your area who have a working relationship with the casting directors. When searching for actors to be in their commercials, casting directors tend to contact talent agents, the people who have a financial incentive (commissions) to represent the talent that is most likely to get the job.

While the structure of commercials has changed over the years, the basic psychology behind them has not. They may be using visual images more than words now, but they are still selling lifestyle more than they are selling products. If you want to get cast in your share of spots, keep the following few guidelines in mind when you arrive at the audition.

1. The implied visual message in most commercials is that if the viewer uses the product being advertised, he will be like the person that appears in the commercial.

This is why nervous actors get knocked out of competition early. If you audition for a commercial and you appear nervous and shy on camera, the implied visual message would be, "If I use this product, I will become nervous and shy." Clearly, that is not what the advertisers want to communicate. If you come across as defensive and unhappy on camera, you can be certain they will move on to the next, happier actor.

2. In commercials, the world is populated by one big, loving, and sometimes goofy family.

Strangers frolic together at the supermarket meat counter, and the server at McDonald's is just like your happy cousin Ella. At a business meeting crazy coworker Larry may get up on the conference table and drink a Pepsi and do a little jig just because he's in a silly mood. A person who washes his car in a commercial is presenting the whole neighborhood with the opportunity for a fun neighborhood water fight. In the world of commercials, there really are not very many strangers. There are only family members you maybe didn't know you had until you arrived at the store.

What this means is that, beginning with the first audition, you need to get directly to the fanny-slapping stage with strangers. Personal space disappears. Stand close enough to smell your acting partner's breath. (Invest in Altoids and Binaca!) In life, we reserve our personal space for intimates and lovers. In commercials, everybody is welcome there. It's a visual image thing. The average television viewer will not be sophisticated enough about the impact of visual images to understand he is being manipulated, but that is in fact what is going on. When we see two people standing close together, we presume they know and probably like one another. Put two strangers at the checkout stand physically close to one another, and you communicate that the world is populated by one big family. The television viewer at home probably feels alienated in a too-fast world, and so the advertising images invite him to be family—if he will only purchase the product being advertised. See how it works?

3. Just because you appear in a commercial does not mean that you personally endorse the product or lifestyle.

A commercial role is a gig, not a personal campaign. My own guideline is that I will appear in a commercial for any product just as long as the product neither physically hurts anybody nor offends me politically. I would not, for example, appear in a commercial for tobacco products. Also, while it personally annoys me that men are depicted as harebrained in most commercials, I figure it's a harmless misrepresentation. Over 60 percent of all commercials target the female consumer, which is why husband/wife relationships in them are typically played as mother/son. The big advertising idea behind it is that women should appear empowered when it comes to the purchasing of household products. In the world of commercials, a man would probably starve unless a woman cooked for him.

Actresses are often offended by commercial stereotypes, and I offer them the same advice. It's just a job! Take the money and use it to support yourself so you can make bigger statements with your art. A commercial audition is no place to get your back out of joint because the woman is washing dishes while the man has his feet up in front of the ball game. If you won't play along, the advertisers will simply move along to the next actress.

4. Actingwise, there is very little conflict in commercials.

Think of commercials as children's theatre instead of *Rashoman* or *Medea*. The people who populate commercials are a low-stress group. You don't get purse snatchings or airplane crashes in commercial-land. A dirty dish is just another opportunity, and people don't get fat if they live on Big Macs. When you go to a commercial audition, leave your worries on the doorstep. Just direct your feet to the sunny side of the street.

Television shows exist in order to deliver good-humored consumers to the commercials. It is incorrect to say that that commercials sponsor the shows. The truth is the other way around; the shows sponsor the commercials.

Maybe you, like me, are a person who thinks we spend *too* much time selling things to one another in America. Maybe you are a woman who bridles at the stereotypical image of females in commercials. If you have reservations about the role of commercials in our society or the psychology behind them, you will have difficulty getting cast. You need to clear your head so that you can be a team player with the ad agency execs. They much prefer to hire actors they perceive to be team players.

I look at commercials this way. As long as the product I'm helping sell doesn't actually hurt anybody, what's the difference? Inside my democratic socialist heart, I might wish things were different. I might wish we in the U.S. didn't put a dollar sign on absolutely everything in life, and I might wish that our government supported the arts so that actors didn't have to do commercials in order to survive. But I would be whistling in the wind. Our economic system is what it is, and the truth is that actors are on their own. If you want to survive and have a shot at the American Dream, you will very likely have to do commercials. Therefore, you would be smart to come to terms with them mentally.

Advertising is about selling happiness, not products. The implied message in most commercials is this: "If you use this product, you will be like the people in the commercial." Almost always, this equates to having a fun sense of humor, a vibrant sex life, a nice home and car, plenty of disposable income, good friends, and cute kids. A commercial is like a snapshot of a happy emotion. This formula has worked since the 1950s, when television advertising was first created by pioneers like David Ogilvy (1987). Trendy advertising campaigns move in and out of favor each television season, mainly so that ad agencies can give statuettes to one another at the Clio Awards, but advertising philosophy always returns to the same baseline. If you want to act in commercials on a regular basis, you need to understand this basic fact of advertising life. The most important thing you can bring to a commercial audition is an optimistic and friendly sense of life. This is far more important than your ability to read copy.

In terms of the shamanistic impulse, a commercial is about embracing the tribe with a big dose of goodwill. It's a love-in, a reach-out-and-touch-someone kind of moment. The actor leads and the audience follows with its checkbook in hand. In fact, you don't even need to be a highly trained actor in order to do commercials. The most important qualification is a winning, energetic sense of life.

Television Shows

American commercial television simultaneously thrills and offends. It is primarily a sales tool masquerading as a pop-culture art form, and its function, as stated above, is to deliver good-humored consumers to the advertising. The technology of television is dazzling and is becoming more so as it merges with the Internet, but program content is too often the visual equivalent of chewing gum or, worse, a narcotic. Nonetheless, the cyber-age actor will be very dependent on television for his livelihood because the United States government does not enthusiastically support the arts. Sweden spends eighty-five dollars per citizen in support of the arts (1995 figures, National Endowment of the Arts), while the United States, which enjoys a much higher gross domestic product, spends six dollars per citizen. France spends fifty-seven dollars per person, Finland ninety-one dollars per person,

Australia twenty-five dollars per person. Of all the civilized countries in the world, the United States spends the least per capita on the arts. Therefore, an actor in America is on his own when it comes to survival. If you can't look to the government or a Medici family for support, then you must look to commerce. Regular employment on a hit television show can bring princely riches, fame, and adoration and, if you are very lucky, artistic satisfaction. Actors on the hit TV show *Friends* made headlines when the entire cast negotiated multimillion-dollar-salary season-renewal packages. Even day-players on television shows can earn sufficient residuals to avoid waiting tables or parking cars. If the twenty-first-century actor's career can be likened to a sea journey, then income from television will be the ballast that keeps the ship from capsizing.

Television is where we Americans advertise our wares and is crucial to the way we elect our political leaders. Television is strategically important to the way we fight our overseas wars (Remember the Gulf War as reported on CNN? It had its own theme song!), and it is how we receive the news of the day. It is our picture window onto the lives of other Americans rich and poor, and it is the twenty-first-century replacement for the potbellied stove in the general store. It should come as no surprise that the average household has its television(s) turned on more than seven hours per day (1998 figures, Nielsen Media Research). Television stars become our friends and soul mates and frequently our dinner dates. The casts of hit television shows are our surrogate neighbors. Television programs are largely responsible for how the average American perceives the U.S. judicial system, allowing him to watch as presidents are impeached, sports heroes stand trial on murder charges, and executions are carried out. They provide our children with role modeling for adulthood and, some would say, desensitize them to violence. They help define our sense of physical beauty as well as our concepts of masculinity and femininity. Leaving aside the judgment about whether such a prominent role for commercial television in American culture is good or bad, the bottom line is that sociologically and in pure dollar terms it is a fact. Try to imagine America without television and you will draw a mental blank. Television has been a part of our reality for the past fifty years and now, with its marriage to the Internet, the medium promises to loom much larger in our lives. Even if you agree with former FCC Commissioner Newton Minnow's famous 1961 description of television as a "vast wasteland," you still must come to terms with it as an actor if you want to pay the rent.

Acting on Television

Acting on most television shows stretches a different set of muscles than does acting on stage because the content of the shows is so homogenized. The mandate of television executives is to sell ad time, and that means that all programming must be calming or reassuring to the viewer, not agitating. Television reaches out to the viewer and treats him much like a camp counselor at a YMCA summer camp would treat the campers. It amuses him, but not to the point that he becomes unruly; it makes him think, but not to the point where his thoughts become unsettling. It saves the ghost stories for the campfire, just before bedtime. Television producers understand when they sign production contracts that their shows must not disturb the viewer or unduly challenge him. An unhappy viewer is not going to be responsive to the commercials. The plot lines of television shows, therefore, tend to feature basic, stereotypical situations with neat and easy solutions to problems. Television casting favors the likeable, nonthreatening actor over the dangerous one. I have acted in hundreds of television shows precisely because I present a nonthreatening, likeable demeanor and because I have the ability to make something out of nothing, regardless of how poorly written the role may be.

Screen Actors Guild statistics indicate that actors earn twice to three times as much from television as they do from movies. Stage income, of course, is miniscule to the point of insignificance. Commercial residuals are the largest source, amounting to over $700 million each year. Employment on the television shows themselves delivers another $350 million or so. The important point is that there are zero indications this will change, even in the cyber future. As long as the United States is a capitalistic society dedicated to commerce over all else, advertising will remain central to the vitality of the economy, and actors will continue to be employed on television. The actor is the human face of American commerce. We are needed for the shows that deliver the consumer to the commercials, and we are needed for the commercials. If television executives could do it without actors, they would. Five of the top ten prime-time shows in June 2000 featured neither actor nor script as the airwaves were awash with "reality" shows. Seventy-five percent of the new programs hitting the air in 2001 will not have actors. But as we have already discussed, the public will not long tolerate a steady diet of reality programming. Role-playing and storytelling are basic to human interaction, and television programs scratch this itch.

For the serious artist, the problem with television is one of aesthetics. Actors who work on television shows and in commercials may be artists, but the function they are filling is sales. Only occasionally do art and commerce intersect. If it became known that priests have to work day jobs in corporate human resources departments in order to afford to preach on Sunday, or that math teachers must moonlight in accounting departments so that they can afford to teach high school, there would be a public outcry. It would be front-page news in the *New York Times* and fodder for Oprah. Sadly, actors are not viewed that way. We are no longer considered essential to the spiritual or educational good health of our culture. We are entertainment, a diversion, a novelty, fun party guests. Indeed, it is a guiding objective of this book that actors must take the initiative in reversing this perception.

Lee Phillips, a good friend of mine and a talented photographer, told me over a couple of cappuccinos recently how difficult it is to express herself as an artist while still earning a living. Sound familiar? In her case, she lives off commercial photography, taking pictures of coffee cups and slices of bacon and bicycles. Her dream is that she will one day sell enough fine-art photography to survive. She would love to follow in the footsteps of Ansel Adams. "I don't want to be a photographic technician," she explained. "I'm an artist. I want to express myself." It is difficult to express yourself when you are being paid to showcase a pair of summer sandals. Lee does it with backgrounds and atmosphere. She takes pride in adding the extra little touches that can evoke emotion even from a picture of a dinner plate.

Actors who work on television shows face a similar challenge. The programs are cranked out at a feeding-frenzy pace, with only one goal: to keep the TV viewer sitting in his chair during commercial break. When producers must turn out twenty-one hours of film in a single season, there is not much opportunity for depth of character. So what is an actor to do? How can you express yourself as an artist while simultaneously functioning as a cog in the giant wheel of television commerce? You do it by staying on the pulpit and by finding small ways to communicate with the audience. You do it by continually searching for points of empathy, insights into the human condition.

The first time I saw actor Al Pacino was on a 1969 TV show entitled *N.Y.P.D.* He played a small-time southern crook as I recall. There was a scene in a hospital in which the two lead cops on the show—Robert Hooks and Frank Converse—were questioning Pacino. Being the bigot that he was, Pacino's character could not stand the idea of being questioned by a black man. His line, which I remember all these many years later, was simple. "I can't talk to you with him in the room," referring to the black actor Robert Hooks. Pacino chose to do something really brilliant and insightful with the line. Instead of spitting out the words as a stereotypical racist of the KKK variety might do, he whispered it to the white cop. He said it as simply and honestly as he would explain that snow falls in the winter. The impact his performance had on me, in the audience, was to give me an insight into the mind of a true bigot, not a pretend one. Racism at its worst is paternal. A black man can ignore or even fight with a white racist who snarls at him. But how to do you fight with someone who dismisses you altogether? What do you do if you are rendered invisible? Pacino's performance rose above the commercialism of television and became art because I was informed by it. I learned something about myself in that moment. Since then, Pacino's star has risen high and he has become one of America's premier actors. His talent was evident even back then, in a single line. I have often thought of that performance; you can tell by my reaction how powerful the moment must have been. I write this in the year 2001. I saw that episode of *N.Y.P.D.* in 1969. You do the math.

Fred Grandy, star of the long-running hit *Love Boat*, and, more recently, a U.S. congressman, likens acting on television to "liquid modeling." Another successful television actor I know says that "acting on television isn't acting. It's something *like* acting." While there are definitely exceptions to this analysis, I think it is a comfortable fit for the overwhelming majority of television programs. My best preparation for work on television came from my early years in New York. When I was a new actor, I acted off Broadway and off-off Broadway. Most of what I did in those days was first productions of original plays, which means I created the characters for the first time. It is a very different experience to portray a character in a Tennessee Williams or Arthur Miller play than it is to portray a character in a new work by an unknown writer. If you are working on Tom in *Glass Menagerie*, you know the play is kitchen-tested. It will work if you can just find the key. With a new play, it is entirely possible that the writing is flawed. This is exactly the situation you encounter when working on television shows. The writing is, at best, mediocre and, at worst, god-awful.

Stage

The good news is that there will still be a place for the low-tech legitimate theatre in the cyber age. There will always be those who enjoy and are stimulated by the live presentation of a good play, and there will always be theatre professionals who, by hook or by crook, will get the curtain up on time. More good news is that the number of regional nonprofit theatres is growing, and their financial health is relatively more robust than it was five years ago. The U.S. economy has been hot for the past several years, primarily due to the Internet, and there has been a trickle-down financial benefit to the thousand-plus nonprofit theatres scattered around the country. They have been able to afford larger-cast productions, reversing a twenty-year downward trend. Patrons have more money to spend on tickets, and the suddenly rich have more money to donate to worthy causes. (Stop me before I get *too* carried away with their motivations, however. Donations to nonprofits are accompanied by tax breaks.)

The challenge for the theatre is twofold: (1) surviving even when the bloom fades from the rose and the hot economy chills, and (2) finding ways to bring theatre to the average person. We have been drifting toward a theatre-only-for-the-wealthy for many years as costs have skyrocketed and movies have siphoned off increasing portions of the audience. Federal support for the theatre has been neither enthusiastic nor ample since the 1930s, and, of course, subsidy is what generally pays the tab when theatre is made available to the lower classes.

Relatively few people can afford to spend $55 and more for a ticket to a Broadway play, or even $25 for a ticket to see regional theatre. Entire segments of the U.S. population are neither participating in nor being nurtured by theatre.

Aside from dependence on continued largess from the rich private and corporate donors plus support from individual city governments, how can the theatre thrive in the cyber age? Though there will be resistance to it from purists, the logical answer is that the theatre will expand its reach, lower the audience common denominator, and raise its profitability via the digital revolution. I can envision not only thriving Internet multiplexes for films, but also the Internet equivalent of the "live" theatre, compliments of digital technology. In the Roman Colosseum, there were 50,000 spectators. Why can't we play to audiences of that size again? The Internet and digital video may very well make it possible to play to the common man. The technological stumbling block is to find a way to approximate the live-theatre experience online, and there are those who will argue it is an impossible and impractical task. Audience members in the live theatre feed off one another, and shifting the live theatre into cyberspace, they will say, is the equivalent to putting Woody Allen movies in IMAX format, a misapplication of technology. As William Gregg, producing artistic director of New American Theatre in Rockford, Illinois, said at a 1999 Theatre Communications Group conference, "We have to restate every day that we are live, that theatre is visceral" (*American Theatre* 2000). This is why comedy is not as funny when seen by people in a sparsely filled auditorium. In the theatre, we seek that feeling of a community gathering. In order to make it work in cyberspace, audience members must somehow have a sense of the real-time response of other audience members scattered around the world. I do not pretend to know the answer yet, but I am unwilling to surrender the battle to the naysayers. The pieces of the puzzle are obviously spread out on the table before us if we can only figure out how to put them together. This being the U.S. of A., it is also true that financial incentive counts for a lot. Entrepreneurs will always chase the money, and there is a lot of it to be made by the first person that can merge the mediums.

If it is true, as I contend, that the stage for actors has expanded through history from a circle drawn in the dirt into a cyber future of cameras and digital interactivity, then it stands to reason that the legitimate theatre must somehow embrace the technology. If it does not, I see no option but to continue the relentless march toward a time when the live theatre is purely the domain of the wealthy. Just imagine what Shakespeare or Molière might have done with this technology!

Jerry Stropnicky, of Pennsylvania's Bloomsburg Theatre Ensemble, also spoke up at that 1999 TCG conference: "We are not mass media; all theatre is local" (*American Theatre* 2000). Mr. Stopnicky is of course correct, but the definition of "local" is changing. Nation-state boundaries are eroding in the cyber age. The long view of human evolution shows that man has always adapted to the technology that is available, or the lack of it. We formed towns and cities because that was the most efficient way to communicate with one another. Electricity gave light to the cities, not the plains. Hot and cold running water first appeared in cities, not on farms. In the twenty-first century, there is light and electricity pretty much everywhere. Humans no longer have to group the way they have traditionally, and so we are witnessing regroupings based on ideas. The "cyber community" is more than a catchphrase. It is increasingly a reality of our time. Watch Europe as it struggles with the Euro economy. Observe Eastern Europe as it divides and reformulates itself. Everywhere, populations are in transit, back and forth across the oceans. As an acting teacher in San Francisco, I can attest to the changes. Time was when 90 percent of my students were Caucasian. Today, almost half of my students are of other ethnic origins, many of them speaking English as a second language. (I can't begin to tell you how much I admire *anybody* who tries to act in English as a second language!) My point is that "local" will in the cyber future be located more in the realm of ideas than within picket fences and city-limits signs. A cyber community may well be comprised of people who live on several different continents, speaking twenty different languages.

In some very immediate ways, there are already a few bridges between the stage and the Internet. There are ways for the legitimate theatre to plug into that global audience. It is possible today, for example, to routinely record plays, probably in multiple camera digital format, for later Internet transmission. Cast members and directors can already be compensated as much for future cyber use as they are for the play's current run. True, this is more of a cross-fertilization than a merger, but when you are measuring the progress of an art form that is nine thousand years old, it must be taken in small increments.

One final note about the legitimate theatre and cyberspace. An Oakland, California, company, DigiScents, Inc., has acquired SenseIT of Herzelia, Israel. Together, these companies plan to endow computers with the ability to emit smells. Clearly, they are motivated by the prospects of enticing prospective automobile buyers with the smell of new leather seats and females with the scent of expensive perfume and grocery shoppers with the aroma of fresh baked bread. However, I can't help but think that this puts us one step closer to the cyber reality of "the smell of the grease paint and the roar of the crowd." Beam me up, Scottie.

Movies

When the average actor thinks of movies, he still imagines big-budget Hollywood productions that will ultimately be exhibited in a cineplex. Given the surge in production of lower-budget movies, especially those shot on digital video, this preconception needs to be updated. The cyber-age actor will not merely wander around with his headshot in his hand, hoping to get in on a hot casting session. He may well be involved in production. This is why actors today should know about more facets of the entertainment industry than just acting. They should know editing, directing, producing, basic cinematography. Citing Buckminster Fuller once again, it is better to be a generalist than a specialist. The cyber-age actor should be a Renaissance person. Not only was da Vinci able paint a pretty decent portrait, but he could also build a catapult, design a flying machine, and divert a river.

The average budget for a conventional 35 mm Hollywood movie is upward of $20 million. In some cases, the movie star alone gets that much money, and there is an additional $20 million spent on actual production! When considered against this background, it becomes clear why digital video movies are shaking the earth on which Hollywood moguls walk. A *big* budget digital video movie is going to cost $500,000 to one million dollars, and it is entirely possible to bring them in for a fraction of that cost. No-budget, seat-of-the-pants movie directors and producers are able to charge the cost of movies on their personal credit cards. Budgets in the $25,000–$75,000 range are as common as a three-leaf clover in the garden these days. Entertainment industry trade papers are chock-full of press releases for new digital production deals and start-up companies. Instead of announcing a single movie, as was typical of the way business was done in the old days, new companies are announcing fifteen and twenty movies, to be produced over a two- or three-year span. It's moviemaking at a totally frenetic pace, and the end result is going to be a lot more work for actors.

Digital video converts visual images into zeros and ones, the language of computers. Once they are in digital form, the images can be imported into computers for editing. They can be uploaded into the Internet for exhibition or transferred from one computer to another. Digital images can be broadcast over television or transferred to videotape. If the digital images recorded have more than five hundred lines per inch, they can easily be transferred to 35 mm for big-screen theatrical distribution.

Digital video is an amazing, almost magical technology, and it would be an understatement to say that executives in the entertainment industry are beside themselves with anxiety and excitement over it. One faction sees digital as a boon to production, and another sees it as a threat. The performing unions, SAG and AFTRA, are trying to figure out what to do about it. If a movie can be copied and traded around so easily, how do the artists keep their hand in the pot?

It is worth remembering that when movies came along at the beginning of the twentieth century, alarmists predicted the death of stage plays. When television appeared, the fear was that this new medium would mean the death of the movie industry. When videotape appeared, making it easy for the consumer to make VHS copies of movies and TV shows, the fear was that people would stop paying to go to the movie theatres. In the music industry, the fear was that audiocassette tapes would cause the end of music royalties for performers and would lead to decreased sales of albums. None of these fears turned out to be justified, and now we have a cyber-age version of the same alarm. As was the case before, fears this time will turn out to be unnecessary. Digital technology will lead to cheaper movie production and easier copying, which will simply increase the excitement of the public and lead to even greater sales. One way or the other, artists will still get paid for their work. Maybe they'll charge more up front, allowing for the "free" copying and trading that may happen later. Maybe there will be some sort of encoding system in digital movies that make duplication without royalty payments very difficult. It doesn't matter really, and it isn't a make-or-break factor in your career strategies as a cyber-age actor. The important thing for you to know is that the cyber-age actor lives in a digital environment. Digital is going to present you with more opportunities to act and to be paid.

When I lived in Hollywood, I occasionally lunched with a producer/director named Henry Jaglom. Henry is an immensely talented man who figured out long ago how to be a one-man show in a mega-studio business. He writes, produces, frequently stars in, and distributes his own movies. Most of his films (*Tracks, Can She Bake a Cherry Pie, New Year's Day, Eating,* to name just a few) are available for rental and are worth a look-see. In fact, anybody who has figured a way to thrive in Hollywood like this is worth a close study.

I mention Jaglom now because he once admonished me for spending too much time chasing talent agents and casting directors. "If you want to be in movies, just write a script, rent a camera, and start shooting," he advised. "Anybody can make a movie. I've been doing it for years." I didn't follow Henry's advice back then, but he is fresh on my mind as digital video rears its head. The fact is that for less than $50,000, you can purchase all the equipment you need to make and edit a full-length movie, and the cost is falling all the time. The first digital video movie to hit the big time was *Blair Witch Project,* shot on a budget of $40,000 and ultimately grossing hundreds of millions of dollars. Once the grosses for *Blair Witch Project* were in, everybody it seems bought a digital camera and started making movies. Production is hard to measure, but it is clearly rampant and includes major names in the industry. People like George Lucas, Spike Lee, and Mike Figgis are shooting digital. There is so much production, in fact, that it has fostered an entirely new kind of platform for exhibition: The Internet multiplex. Instead of driving to the cineplex, the movie lover will soon be able to download and watch movies at home on demand directly from the Internet. He can already do it actually, but the process will accelerate, and the movies will get longer and more lavish as faster-speed access replaces the current 56K modem speed. The wave of the future is the DSL line and ISDN, both of which promise super-fast download.

Perhaps for the foreseeable future, actors will continue to be colors on a director's palette, but we now have the option of creating our own palette, too. Some actors are going to make their own movies and, in doing so, will attract much attention. It's not as expensive as you might think. For $50,000, you can purchase equipment that is sufficiently high-end to shoot and edit a full-tilt feature film now. If you are budget-minded, you can do it for as little as $10,000. Here's a shopping list:

- A three-chip digital video camera (Sony and Canon are the most popular) costs approximately $2,000. You can get by with a less expensive single-chip camera, which costs half that amount.
- A high-end Apple Macintosh computer that can easily handle graphics costs $4,000.
- A high-end monitor (computer screen) costs starting from $1,500 and up.
- The editing software favored by many Hollywood moviemakers is Final Cut Pro, which costs $900.
- You'll need additional external hard drives (the more the merrier) to attach to your computer because digital editing takes up a lot of space on your computer. In fact, asking your computer to handle digital editing is perhaps the most demanding chore it can handle. Forty-gigabyte external hard drives with Firewire connections to your computer cost approximately $500 at the low end.

You can get by without sophisticated lighting for digital moviemaking because the cameras are so sensitive. Typically, the standard light in a room will suffice. You'll need special lights for nighttime shooting and for interior directional lighting, but none of this is very expensive, measured in the hundreds of dollars, not thousands.

Once you own the equipment, you may need some training to learn how to operate it, but the beauty of digital is that it is user friendly. The most difficult thing to master is probably Final Cut Pro. Training for that software could cost you another $1,000. So you can see that, given you have a story to tell and the ability to get a script written, the technical side of moviemaking is now within your control and your pocketbook.

Are you beginning to see why I said in the first sentence of this book that the cyber age is an exciting time to be an actor? Every serious cyber-age actor should have basic moviemaking knowledge. He should own a fast computer, be Internet savvy, and have access to a digital camera. He should remain abreast of exhibition platforms and make it his business to watch new digital movies the same way he watches new productions of stage plays. Technological advances are going to come down at breakneck speed, and the actor needs to stay in the loop. In addition to our regular subscriptions to industry trade publications like *Daily Variety, Hollywood Reporter,* and *Backstage West-DramaLogue*, the cyber-age actor should regularly read publications devoted to digital technology. *Wired* magazine, for example, is a must-read, as is *RES*, a magazine specifically about digital filmmaking.

In addition to acting training, the cyber-age actor should have a basic knowledge of editing techniques. Many universities are offering this training now, and there are nonprofit organizations such as the Film Arts Foundation (<www.filmarts.org>) in San Francisco that offer low-cost classes in the subject.

Acting in Movies

An actor creates a stage performance in the present moment, either by herself or in concert with other actors, and feedback from the audience is immediate. Her performance on film, by contrast, is created in the editing room in collaboration with the director and editor, and audience feedback is nonexistent. For some actors, these differences become almost insurmountable challenges. Many excellent stage actors become frustrated and tense with the demands of film production. It is essential that the cyber-age actor not fall into this trap because he is going to spend far more time in front of cameras than did twentieth-century actors.

A movie scene is constructed this way: The director records the action and dialogue from various perspectives. Typically, he begins with a master shot, which is a single shot that encompasses all of the actors and 100 percent of the action in the scene. Then the actors play the scene again while the director records *coverage*, close-ups this way and close-ups that way. He may record *inserts*, separate shots of hands opening drawers, guns being pulled from holsters, letters being written, birds flying overhead, and so on. The camera may be stationary or in motion, and the angles may be high, from above the heads, or low, from the hip. The cast and crew might spend the better part of a day working on a single one-minute scene, having the actors go through the action again and again. Every time the camera moves to a new perspective, the scene must be relit and restaged, and backgrounds must be adjusted for continuity and consistency. Later, after all of the film has been developed, the director and editor sit down at an editing table and piece all of these perspectives together so that they appear to present a scene in real-time. The audience doesn't care that Actor A's reaction to Actor B's line was recorded after the lunch break. Indeed, the audience doesn't even want to *think* about such things.

An actor working in a movie must adjust to this drawn-out production rhythm. He must let it wash over him like a warm bath. If it makes him nervous, the camera will see the tension, presenting the editor with fewer options in the editing room. He must get into sync with the director and cinematographer, knowing that his ultimate performance will be cobbled together in editing, maybe weeks or months later.

Given the demands of filmmaking, you can probably see why the ideal movie actor is self-confident, poised, and has a yogilike ability to remain focused in the midst of constant distraction. He must also be able to sustain the energy in a scene so that the fifteenth take is as intense as were the first two. If the scene is set in a noisy place such as a cafeteria or bar, the actor has the added challenge of matching his performance energy to the supposed noise level of the background. I say "supposed" level because, when the camera is rolling, that bar room full of extras will be made to act silently, to walk around in stocking feet, to make no noise at all. The director wants to capture a clean recording of the actor's voices. The jukebox in the corner will not be playing a song that sets the mood of the scene, and the bartender will not be clanging liquor bottles into one another. All of that will be added to the scene later, in the editing room.

I have been teaching film classes for actors for many years and have noticed certain recurring misconceptions among new students, the primary one being the notion that movie acting should be "smaller" than stage acting. Another common error is the idea that good movie acting equates to nothing more than an ability to read lines in a relaxed and natural fashion. Smallness, in fact, has nothing whatever to do with film acting. Indeed, if an actor makes his performance small, he invariably makes it less important and winds up boring the audience. And neither does smallness equate to naturalness.

Let's pick up a theme that has been with us since the start of this book. Actors are storytellers. You tell your story from the perspective of a circle drawn in the dirt or from the proscenium arch or from the sound stage. Regardless of the medium or the distance from the audience, storytelling requires theatrical intent on the part of the actor. The reason you are acting in a movie is to tell a story. The only functional difference between stage and film really is that the story told on stage is told by the actors alone, and the story told on film is told by a consortium of people, including the director. The actor has total control of the stage performance, but the editor and director have ultimate total control of the film performance. In this respect, the story told on film involves more collaboration than the one told on stage.

One of the unique things about movies is that the camera shows the audience exquisitely nuanced detail in the acting plus a true image of real locations. In the theatre, an audience can see a single leafless tree center stage and imagine an entire barren landscape. In the movies, no imagination is necessary. The scene was shot in the desert, near a single leafless tree. In movies, the audience accepts the locations for what they are and focuses on the interplay between actors. There is another striking difference between stage and film: On stage, the audience tends to watch the person who is talking, and on film it tends to watch the person who is listening.

In the Academy Award–winning movie *The English Patient*, Juliette Binoche and Ralph Fiennes play a scene in which Fiennes' character dies after Binoche's character administers to him a lethal dose of morphine. As his final moments fade, the camera watches Binoche, who is reading a book to him. She glances up from the book, her eye stopping on the off-screen actor. We can tell by her expression and her thoughts that the man has at that very instant passed away. Then the editor cuts to an image of Fiennes lying lifeless. The shot of him is included simply to verify that what we saw in Binoche's expression was true. The man died. My point is that if this scene were played on stage, the audience would very probably have been watching Fiennes, not Binoche. In the movies, we tend to follow events largely through the reactions of the characters involved.

I recall watching Julie Harris on Broadway in *The Last Days of Mrs. Lincoln*. At the end of the play, she sat in a chair and died. At the moment of death, there was another character on stage, talking to her. It was a bravura moment of acting because you could see her body suddenly become heavier in that chair as her last breath escaped her lips. She sank in upon herself, seemed to become smaller and heavier. The point of focus on stage was Ms. Harris, not the woman who was talking to her. When we saw Harris die, we shifted our gaze to the talking character to see if she saw what we saw. If the scene had been shot for the movies, our focus would have been the other way around.

The camera sees thoughts. Think it, and it's done. Yes, a scene still should have conflict, obstacles, and negotiations and, yes, the actors should still play actions in pursuit of objectives. But the closer the camera gets, the more it sees the thoughts. A good film actor will adjust to this reality, allowing the camera to become intimate with him. Michael Caine, in his marvelous book *Acting in Film: An Actor's Take on Movie Making,* says that the actor should think of the camera as a lover who will forgive him anything. I think that is a marvelous metaphor.

Adrenaline Moments

Scientists have figured out why we humans remember important events in our lives. I can tell you very precisely where I was the moment I received word that John Kennedy had been assassinated. I recall the time of day, the temperature in the airline terminal where I heard the news bulletin, the face of the shoeshine man whose radio it was. We all can remember the first time we made love. It may not have been pretty, but we can remember it. I was there when my daughter, Dagny, was born, and I still get an emotional rush when I describe the event.

It turns out that when something really significant happens to us, whether it is good news or bad, our brains get drenched with adrenaline. It is nature's way of saying, "Remember this! It is important!" It is part of our basic survival mechanisms. The first time you see a friend get eaten by a saber-tooth tiger, nature says you should remember the danger. That way, the next time you see one of those tigers, you'll know to run the other direction.

Good acting consists of adrenaline moments. Think about it: You want to tell a story in as efficiently and compelling a manner as possible, right? You pick the parts of the story that carry the most voltage when you do the telling. A scene must be worthy of the audience's time. Shakespeare had a marvelous handle on this principle. In his plays, if the guy doesn't get the girl, France might fall! An audience does not want to see a common love affair or a common moment. It wants to see an extraordinary love affair and the moment when Juliet drinks the poison. It wants to see Anthony and Cleopatra, Benedick and Beatrice. Regardless of the scene, the actor should play it as if it matters.

I define an adrenaline moment as one that the characters will remember when they turn eighty-five and reflect on their lives. "I remember the day I first met your grandma," Grandpa begins. Or "It was a close call. The engine on the right side of the airplane just quit all of a sudden, and we began to fall from the sky."

This, then, is the answer to the misconception about movie acting being "small." Smallness is not the issue, importance is. The scene should have significance, even if the action is distilled into an extreme close-up of a woman's eyes, slightly shifting at the moment she notices the man lying on the bed pass into death. Nothing could be smaller than Juliette Binoche's flickering thought at that moment in *The English Patient*, and nothing could be more significant.

Computer Games

Have you ever had an audition for a computer game? It's a wild experience. In the first place the script for a computer game is severely disjointed because the ultimate audience is a game player who will interact with the game. Typically, Character #1 will run into the picture and yell, "Which way should we go, Captain? The meteor is upon us!" The player selects a direction, and the game takes off on a new tangent. If the player had selected a different direction, the game would have gone a whole other way. And so the auditions for computer games consist of very short verbal exchanges, combined with physical action.

Most computer games are still the realm of animated characters, but this is changing rapidly. As soon as the average game player has powerful enough access, computer games will live in the Internet, available for quick downloading. When play is complete, the game will be returned to its Internet shelf. Characters may be animated or live-action, or a combination of the two. For a harbinger of the future of computer games, look closely at the *Star Wars* movies. Imagine, if you could, with your little joystick, controlling Luke Skywalker as he does battle with the dark forces.

Computer games provide employment for actors in several ways. The obvious one is live-action, as I have just described. Then there are the voices for animated characters and creatures. And, finally, there is the world of motion-capture, an amazing technique in which actors are placed in electrode-encrusted harnesses and navigated around an area approximately the size of a boxing ring. The electrodes are hooked up to computers so that images on a computer screen move in concert with the actor's movement. If the actor lifts his left arm, the thing on the screen lifts its left arm. Or tentacle. If the actor crouches, the thing crouches. Clearly, working as a motion-capture artist requires a specialized skill, but that only means that it is one more skill for the cyber-age actor to master. Check the Internet to find companies that specialize in motion-capture production. You'll find them in the major entertainment industry markets. Call them up, ask what you can do to be included. Meanwhile, if you want to read the definitive book on this subject, check out *Understanding Motion Capture for Computer Animation and Video Games* by Alberto Menache (2000). The intended readers for his book are animators and special effects artists, but the information in there will help you as an actor understand what is involved.

Cyber Tools

The twenty-first-century actor should, at minimum, own a computer and photo scanner. He should also have an Internet presence to go along with his customary eight-by-ten headshot and résumé, which means his own website.

Heinemann published a useful book entitled *The Actor's Guide to the Internet* by Rob Hozlowski (2000), which is an excellent primer on the Internet for the newly wired. Mr. Hozlowski gets into the technical side of things, walking you through the step-by-step process of going online and building your own website, and so I defer to him. For now, we will stick to online career strategies.

The reason you need a computer and photo scanner is that actors increasingly have the opportunity to submit their photo and résumé over the Internet. I have on my desk at this moment a casting notice I received from a film director. His project is entitled "Dating for the Masses," and he has set up a website so actors can learn more about it. In his notice, the director says, "We love online headshots, so if you have such a thing, you can either send us the web address or attach it to an e-mail at [his e-mail address]. Or, if you are a nostalgic snail-mail user, you can send us a copy at . . ." *Snail mail.* That affectionate description of the U.S. Postal Service alone should give the cyber actor plenty of reason to get wired up. In the future, this is largely how business will be conducted.

A scanner is a kind of fax machine–copier that you attach to your computer. You can scan your headshot into your computer, converting the visual image into zeros and ones. Then you can attach the scanned image to an e-mail, submitting it to casting directors, directors, or whoever might want it. This is a good reason, by the way, to invest in some color photos in addition to the standard-issue black-and-white headshot. The Internet is a color medium, and you might as well take advantage of it. Since many digital video projects are low budget (or even no budget), the producers do not have the money to attract the participation of talent agents. Instead, they will search for actors in other ways, calling local acting teachers perhaps to ask for recommendations, and putting up a production website to solicit direct submissions from actors.

The reason you personally need a website is so you can refer casting directors, agents, directors, and interested others to it. A website is an extension of your portfolio and can be a valuable promotional tool. You can put your website address, known as a URL, on your paper résumé, right underneath your telephone number. A person who likes your résumé and headshot may go to your website for a more in-depth look at you. It is even possible now to put a digitally recorded audition scene on your site, so that with a fast-enough computer, a browser can download it for casting consideration.

Once you have built your website, I suggest that you begin writing a monthly newsletter in which you report on your theatrical and personal activities and maybe even write editorials about life and art from your point of view. First you send out the newsletter via e-mail to whoever wants to be on your mailing list, and then you post it to your website so that visitors there can see it. I write two such newsletters each month in connection with my acting workshops. One is for regular actors through my website <www.edhooks.com>, and the other is for animators through my website <actingforanimators.com>. My mailing lists now contain the addresses of literally thousands of people from all over the world who are interested in my activities. In my view, the personal newsletter, sent via the Internet, is increasingly going to be a primary means of communicating in the cyber age. And don't forget that you can attach a scanned digital photo to your newsletter. Like your mom said, pictures speak louder than words.

Most Internet Service Providers (ISPs) will, for a small charge, "host" your website. Many ISPs include space for websites in their basic monthly charge. My ISP works like that, and I invite you to check out my personal website at <www.edhooks.com>. Generally, the least expensive way for you to develop your own website is through your own ISP. However, there are many Internet-based businesses that will do it for you. These businesses will typically offer a potpourri of services to actors, including access to "sides" and perhaps a presence in a digital database. As I explain elsewhere in this book, money spent on digital databases may be a waste. The lure for inclusion is the suggestion that casting directors will surf the databases when doing casting, but this is not the way the business works. When casting directors are casting money-paying jobs, they tend to call talent agents. They do not log on and start surfing digital databases. Therefore, my recommendation to you is that you develop your own website, at your own expense, and promote it in your own way. That is how you will get the best bang for your cyber buck.

Sides on the Internet

In the horse-and-buggy days, when an actor got an audition, he would either personally go to the casting office to pick up the *sides* (pages from the script), or they would be faxed to him. Today, he has the option of subscribing to a service such as ShowFax (<www.showfax.com>). For a reasonable yearly fee, ShowFax makes available hundreds and hundreds of sides for immediate downloading. Let's say you get an audition for an episodic TV show. Your agent calls with the appointment time and tells you that sides are available at ShowFax. You log on, click on the show's name, and voila! You can download not only the sides for your role, but those for all the other roles, which will give you an even better idea of the show's flavor. You can literally have the script pages in your hands within minutes of receiving the audition call. I subscribe to ShowFax myself and most highly recommend it to you.

Newsgroups and Listservs

When you go online, you will have access to free discussion groups where actors congregate. Some of them function sort of like public bulletin boards, where people leave messages for one another, and some are more personalized. The main newsgroup for actors is <alt.acting>, and a valuable listserv is Acting-Pro. The thing to keep in mind about newsgroups is that, while they can be a valuable source of information, you get what you pay for. The newsgroups can be a promotional venue for the unscrupulous entrepreneur who is intent on selling things to actors. A casting notice in a newsgroup might turn out to be a come-on for pornography, for instance. My advice is that you become an active participant in the newsgroups, but do not leave your good judgment at the cyber door.

Cyber Shovels

During California's early gold gush days, the big fortunes were not made by the miners but by those who sold them shovels. The twenty-first-century actor has much in common with those miners. He too works hard, dreams big, and is an eternal optimist. Just as the gold miner hoped for the big strike, actors hope for the big break. "Just one good part," goes the reasoning, "and I'm never looking back!" Like the forty-niners, the actor is fueled by hopes and dreams.

There is a certain breed of entrepreneur that has a nose for dreams. He can smell them half a mile away, and he rushes to set up a map-to-the-mines shop where the dreamers will be sure to pass by. He decorates his store windows with shiny shovels and pictures of other happy miners who have struck gold, and then he stands in the doorway of his shop with a big grin on his face and a fistful of maps. "I know the way," he says to the dreamers. "Step right in and let me help you find the gold. It doesn't cost much." Hollywood and New York in particular are chock-full of shops like this, and many of them have branch offices in smaller cities. If you dream of acting, there is every likelihood that you will be tempted at some point by an entrepreneur who is hawking maps.

CD Workshops

The cyber version of the map to the mines is the casting director (CD) workshop. Casting directors work for producers, and their job is to go out into the world to find actors. Because they are in a position to broker acting jobs, they are in a position to exploit aspiring actors. This is what the old "casting couch" was all about. The casting director workshop is a more sanitized version of the casting couch. Actors pay money for access to the casting directors, with the hope that such access will result in auditions and, ultimately, paid acting work.

CD workshops are a dime a dozen in major markets, and they all work basically the same way. For a fee, say $25–$35 per three-hour workshop, the actor gets face time with an actual dyed-in-the-wool casting director. The man grinning in the doorway will tell you that you are paying for education, a class in audition technique, but all you really care about is getting access to that casting director. Your dream is that you will be discovered, that you will finally strike gold, that you will not have to face any more dark and empty mine shafts. Rejection comes with an acting career just as white comes with snow. It wears you down, makes you desperate, and causes you to be susceptible to the lure of fool's gold. You know it, the casting director knows it, and the grinning man with the fistful of maps knows it. However, all parties involved agree not to talk about it as you step inside and reach for your checkbook.

The casting director workshop (showcase) first appeared in the 1970s in New York and quickly spread to Hollywood, where it became a cottage industry. Some casting directors reportedly began earning more from workshops than they earned from casting. Because casting directors are not licensed by the state in which they operate the way that talent agents are, they can do pretty much whatever they want to with actors, short of inflicting actual bodily harm. It is not illegal to sell maps to the mines, and it is not illegal to sell access to oneself. In order to appear above the crass commercialism of it all, the casting directors who sell themselves at these workshops depend on entrepreneurs to give the transactions a sheen of legitimacy. The truth is, however, that when you write a check to the promoter of a casting director workshop, he and the CD are splitting the money. They are there for the bucks, not for the opportunity to discover new miners.

As timing would have it, on the very day I was working on this chapter, I received an e-mail from an actor who had just returned home after spending the day in a casting director workshop. This particular event occurred in San Francisco, a regular pit stop for Hollywood and New York casting directors. She told me that the casting director, a well-known lady from New York "with many film credits under her belt," spent the day telling her students that they are not ready yet to be playing lead roles. The actors in New York are so much better prepared, you see. According to my correspondent, the CD allowed as how the hapless San Francisco crowd might be ready for some day-player roles, supporting stuff. And then she devoted some time to "tearing apart the résumés of everybody in the room." The actor felt appropriately chastened, thanked the good CD for telling it like it is, and made a commitment to "keep working at this until I am ready for the good roles."

I wrote back to that actor and assured her that she already was ready for lead roles, that she should not buy into the casting director's game. What possible good does it do a new actor to tell her that she is inadequate, other than to stoke the fragile ego of the casting director? The net result of such treatment is to perpetuate the actor's subservient posture and keep her writing those checks. It was not necessary for that New York casting director to denigrate the San Francisco actors. It was not necessary to tell them they were not ready for prime time. It was not only unnecessary, I will argue that it was cruel. The actors who signed up for this person's workshop did so with their hearts on their sleeves. Indeed, they almost assuredly had an incorrect idea about how the business of casting actually happens, and they probably thought there was a chance they could get discovered, but the prevailing attitude they took into the classroom was hope and good will. This casting director took the opportunity to step on their necks as she cashed their checks.

CD showcases offer 10 percent education and 90 percent hope of being discovered. Actors are not proud of purchasing favor and, when the strategy fails to produce acting work, as is almost always the case, the actors simply slink off into the darkness from whence they came. The organization of casting directors, known as the Casting Society of America (CSA), could put brakes on the showcase activities of its members but, if it tried to do so, the organization itself would probably fold. CSA members are deeply dependent on income from showcases. The Association of Talent Agents (ATA) could protest, but again, the status quo is in its best interest. Actors who grease the palms of casting directors also are greasing the communication between the agents and casting directors.

New actors can be forgiven for concluding that a casting director— a person with day-to-day knowledge of the acting industry—might be the best person to teach acting. There is appealing logic in it if one can learn about acting and getting acting jobs while simultaneously meeting important people in the industry. Teaching is, however, a very special skill. The fact that a person may be a casting director lends close to zero voltage to his value as a teacher.

Digital Databases

Via the Internet, entrepreneurs are offering actors, for a fee, the opportunity to post their photos and résumés and sometimes even digitally videotaped demo scenes online. In order to lure actors into writing the checks, the entrepreneurs typically will suggest, either overtly or subtly, that pictures posted in the databases will attract the attention of important casting directors and agents. My strong advice is that you not be so quick to write those checks if your motive is to showcase yourself. In truth, big-time casting directors do not need to surf the Internet and browse through digital databases in search of actors. If a paying acting job is on the table, the casting director will virtually always contact talent agents, people who have a financial incentive to represent the best available talent in a given market. The only incentive a casting director might have to scan the databases is if the acting job pays no money; or if the casting requirement is so unusual that it is unlikely that candidates would find mainstream agency representation—for example, actors who are over seven feet tall, who might not be represented by regular agents. An agent would be reluctant to add such a person to his client list because there are going to be very few opportunities to make money with him.

Most of the major actor-database companies are located in Hollywood and New York, but you will find bush-league versions of them in smaller cities. There you will encounter local casting directors that are looking for ways to augment their income in a market where there is not enough acting work to justify their presence as full-time casting directors. They will typically establish a digital casting system and charge a nonunion actor a fee to be included. Being a small market, there is some muscle behind the fee. The veiled threat is that, if you don't pay to get yourself included, you won't be considered for casting. It's a cynical business, in my opinion. My advice, if you are living in a city that has this kind of setup, is to focus your energies on getting a good agent. Actors who are represented that way usually are not charged any fees. And, as I explained, when money-paying acting work is at stake, the casting director is going to call talent agents anyway.

Predicting the Cyber Future

Developments in Cyberspace

Progress in cyberspace is taking place so rapidly that predictions about the future may well appear to be a history lesson by the time they are printed. Nonetheless, we actors must keep an eye on the distant horizon, and we must keep our bags packed for the journey. With that future in mind, consider the implications of the following recent cyber developments.

By the year 2004, American homes will have access to about 132 channels on their TV sets, up from 90 channels in 1999. That means more programming will be needed, and that means more work for actors.

Miramax Films is the first major movie studio to release a full-length feature film for download over the Internet. The film, entitled *Guinevere*, was produced in 1999 and stars Stephen Rae and Sarah Polley. For a fee of $3.49, a person can download the film and view it for a twenty-four-hour period—approximately the same fee that he would pay if renting a videotape copy of the film at, say, Blockbuster.

Microsoft has announced the introduction of Solo2, a computer microchip that is designed to deeply intermingle the functions of television and the computer. Solo2 combines, on a tiny sliver of silicon, digital video recording, interactive television, and Internet features. It will allow a TV viewer to surf the web on a television set and watch or record two different programs simultaneously. The chip contains an integrated digital-to-analog converter for direct display of digital content to the television. If Solo2 doesn't impress you, consider this: Before the new chip is even available on the market, Microsoft is already working with the technical team at WebTV to develop a more advanced microchip, one that holds 9 million transistors. (Solo2 holds a mere 2.2 million.)

AOL, the granddaddy of all Internet Service Providers (ISPs), is also offering more services that combine television and the Internet. Intel, the giant chip-manufacturing behemoth, is gearing up for the production of a new generation of microchips that foster the same TV/Internet/Digital/Analog symmetry.

A stand-up comic named Wayne Brady has adapted his personal website in a way that allows home computer users to literally, verbally improvise with him online. He does it by combining new software called HearMe with animations from a company called Macromedia. It may be a short-lived experiment, but the fact that such a thing can be done at all is amazing—and it is a harbinger. When audiences can interact in a real-time way with performers on stage, whether it is through a computer, a television broadcast, or a stage play, you have theatre. Once the shift from passive mass entertainment to interactive mass entertainment is complete, we will see the beginnings of yet another platform for the actor.

It really doesn't matter if Microsoft, WebTV, or Intel hits pay dirt with these new ventures. We're not seeking here to develop a stock portfolio but to understand how actors can profit from the developing revolution. How can we increase our opportunities for artistic expression and enhance our earning power? The important thing for actors to keep in mind is that, one way or another, television and computers are becoming a single unit, and it will happen sooner rather than later. This means that the way network programming has been developed and distributed in the past will change in the future. The television viewer will at some point not be bound by *TV Guide*–style airdate schedules at all. If he wants to watch a particular show, he will click a couple of buttons on a remote control device in his living room or bedroom, or perhaps on a remote he carries with him, and the program will be retrieved from cyberspace for immediate display. This program might be only seconds old, or it might be thirty years old. The distinction between "live" broadcasting and "prerecorded" broadcasting will blur. Digital duplication will make the five hundredth copy of a program just as sharp as the first.

The Actor, the Internet, and the Audience

The Internet is transforming the world into a potential vast new global audience. According to the United States Internet Council, more than 300 million people worldwide now use the Internet, fewer than half of them in North America (*San Jose Mercury News*, 2 September 2000). At the present moment, most people who surf the Net are English speakers, but we are heading for the time when the Chinese can speak directly to the English and the French can speak directly to the Russians in real time. Perhaps it will develop that we can communicate via subtitles, or perhaps there will be on-the-spot audio translators. Whatever the means of contact, when individuals in Africa can join with individuals from Italy, Singapore, India, and Ireland as audience members for a single theatrical event that originates in the Czech Republic or Australia, we will have arrived at a whole new paradigm for the arts. The transaction that began nine thousand years ago with a circle drawn in the dirt and grew through the amphitheatres of Greece and into the twentieth-century motion picture and television industry will once again expand. We are indeed a global village, and even Shakespeare would be impressed. John Perry Barlow, cofounder of the influential think-tank known as the Electronic Frontier Foundation, underlines this thesis when he writes, "I imagine electronically defined venues, where minds residing in bodies scattered all over the planet are admitted, either by subscription or a ticket at a time, into the real-time presence of the creative act. I imagine actual storytelling making a comeback. Storytelling, unlike the one-way, asymmetrical thing that goes by the name in Hollywood, is highly participatory. Instead of 'the viewer' sitting there, mouth slack with one hand on a Bud while the TV blows poisonous electronics at him, I imagine people actually engaged in the process, and quite willing to pay for it" (2000, 240).

The number of online, live-action commercials will increase proportionate to broadband, that is, super-fast download capability. DSL and ISDN connections increase the potential audience of viewers for online ads. Right now, most advertising on the Internet is either animated or banner style. Banner ads are really a cyber version of magazine and newspaper print advertising, and research shows they are inefficient. Only 0.5 percent of the people who view a banner ad on the Internet actually click on it. Also, banner ads are a weak way to establish brand dominance. TV viewers have strong recall of the brand names they see in commercials, but Internet users have very weak recall of brand names they see in banner ads. What this means is that advertising on the Internet will become increasingly live-action. The holdup is only in the access speeds of the computer users.

The current crop of banner ads may feature some simple repetitive movement, like a clock pendulum ticking back and forth or a person picking up a coin, but they are still closer to print than to broadcast. One day, live-action will be the primary type of Internet advertising. Last year, Screen Actors Guild and AFTRA conducted the longest labor strike in their history, against the advertising industry. Significantly, the advertisers did not want to even talk about Internet use, let alone negotiate a contract for actor compensation. They understandably preferred to restrict the talk to network and cable use, the dinosaurs of exhibition. Within the next fifteen years or so, the number of commercials produced directly for the Internet will explode. Income from this source will be critically important to actors. Online advertising revenue is expected to reach $16.5 billion by 2005, according to research conducted by Jupiter Communications. By that time, computer users will be exposed to 950 online ads per day (*Daily Variety*, 17 August 2000).

Two different companies, Eastman Kodak and Foveon, have announced they are going to manufacture a digital chip for still photography that delivers an image with roughly twice the resolution of 35 mm film. This will quickly find its way into digital video, kicking production there into an even more frenzied tempo. "Both companies' achievements have startled industry experts because the new devices move far beyond the current industry standards . . . which until now have been able to achieve resolutions of 6 million pixels a square inch. The Foveon and Kodak sensors can pack 16.8 million pixels into a square inch" (*New York Times*, 11 September 2000).

Digital Actors Versus Real Ones

In addition to teaching acting classes to actors, I have, since 1996, taught acting to animators all over the world. Computer artists create and manipulate 2-D (hand-drawn) and 3-D (computer-generated) characters for movies (*Antz, Toy Story, The Iron Giant*) and television shows (*P.J.'s*) and computer games (Abe's World). You may not have thought much about it before, but animated characters in movies must act and play scenes with one another just like human actors do. As computer animation becomes more sophisticated (*Antz, Toy Story*), audiences come to expect more from it actingwise. I wrote a book, *Acting for Animators* (2000a), on this subject. If you'd like to learn more, check it out.

I'm bringing up the subject of animation now because there is a lot of industry speculation about whether or not a digitally created character can ever replace a flesh-and-blood actor in a lead role. You can see where this idea might appeal to movie producers. An animated actor would work overtime, wouldn't talk back, and wouldn't get residuals. The good news for actors is that it is not going to happen, at least not for lead roles, and certainly not in the foreseeable future. It won't happen because we humans are too complex to duplicate and because we like to see our own kind playing the roles. We delight in mimesis. When animated characters appear on screen, even ultrarealistic ones, an audience member must make an extra mental adjustment in order to suspend his disbelief and be swept along by the story. We can sort of play along with a well-designed computer-generated character in a movie, but it is impossible for us to forget that we are looking at lines and pixels.

Computer animation is being used successfully to flesh out large-scale crowd scenes in movies like *Titanic* and *Gladiator,* and it can be used to trick an audience's eye for a fleeting moment when dangerous stunts are involved on screen. Realistic digital characters, however, cannot withstand audience scrutiny if brought into the foreground and made to play complex scenes. Human actors will always have an edge over computer-generated characters for the simple reason that humans long to relate to other humans, and we do it via emotion and empathy.

As further evidence of how far removed some of us have come from our shaman roots, consider the comment of Screen Actors Guild staffer Allen Weingartner, who was asked in an interview about the prospect of animated actors replacing real ones. "There's sort of a human spark that they [live actors] have that a digital character can't provide" (*San Jose Mercury News,* 31 August 2000). That is an astounding understatement, especially amazing coming from a spokesperson for professional actors. A "sort of" human spark? There is nothing "sort of" about it! The "human spark" is what acting is all

97

about. It is the first and the last word on the subject and between audience and performer is called *empathy*.

Challenges for Ethnic Minority Actors

The hipbone is connected to the thighbone. The cyber-age actor is going to be dependent on television for his livelihood. Television execs will try to produce programming that will deliver to the advertisers the consumers that are the most likely to spend money.

The hot target for television programmers is the eighteen- to forty-eight-year-old female because women are more frequent impulse shoppers than men are, and they tend to be more stylish. A woman will replace her wardrobe as fashions change, but men wear the same suit year after year.

Ethnic minorities are underrepresented on television shows because advertisers do not consider them to be big spenders. Screen Actors Guild reported in May 1999 that the percentage of roles going to African Americans, Latinos, and Native Americans declined from 1997, and they were already low. SAG lobbies continually with television producers, trying to make them cast more actors of color. The goal is to have the casts of television shows more accurately reflect the racial face of America, but it is an uphill battle. TV industry execs would like to include more ethnic minorities; their problem is that doing so is beside the point from a commerce perspective. Their mandate is to draw in the advertisers, and if the advertisers aren't interested in selling to, say, Hispanics, then including Hispanics in the casts of shows won't be helpful. Indeed, the producers might conclude it would be counterproductive. It's all about money. Art and fairness and equality have nothing to do with it.

The good news is that the fast-growing segments of the U.S. population are ethnic minorities, particularly Hispanic and Asian American. Advertisers will increasingly target these groups, which will result in more roles for ethnic-minority actors. Though there was a downswing between 1997 and 1999, the general long-term trend is up.

The ethnic-minority cyber-age actor can do several things to increase his casting opportunities:

1. Take advantage of the digital revolution. Make movies. Be an actor-entrepreneur. Express yourself in ways that are not dependent on advertisers as much as you can.
2. Keep the pressure on television producers and corporate America. This means getting involved with the performing unions and their committees as soon as possible. Volunteer for committees. Support the Non-Traditional Casting Project (NTCP), a not-for-profit advocacy organization established in 1986 to address and seek solutions to the problems of racism and exclusion in theatre, film, and television. NTCP maintains files of photos and résumés in New York and has an Internet presence (Artists Files Online). The organization's work involves (1) advocacy in shaping policy in the profession toward a more inclusive standard, (2) consciousness raising and education, and (3) specific programs through which producers, directors, and casting directors can implement inclusion. You can contact NTCP at the following:

   Non-Traditional Casting Project, Inc.
   1560 Broadway
   Suite 1600
   New York, NY 10036
   (212) 730-4750 Voice
   (212) 730-4913 TDD
   (212) 730-4820 Fax

Background Performers (Extra Work)

Cecil B. DeMille employed extras in *The Squaw Man* (1914), the first Hollywood movie ever shot. Hollywood lore includes plenty of tales of movie stars who "got started working as an extra." The problem is that in 1946 people who worked primarily as extras in Hollywood movies broke off from the Screen Actors Guild and formed their own union, the Screen Extras Guild. From that point on, it was generally understood in the entertainment industry that extras and actors filled two distinct but complementary job functions. There were actors, and there were professional extras. Then, in 1992—after being voted down three different times by members of Screen Actors Guild—extra players were folded back into SAG, and the beleaguered Screen Extras Guild was dissolved.

SAG has never known precisely what to do with extra players. In the premiere issue of SAG's first member magazine, published March 15, 1934, SAG President Eddie Cantor included extras in the broad category of actors when he wrote: "The Screen Actors Guild is, as far as I know, the first organization of all the actors in Hollywood. It was born of the realization that the high-salaried star and the struggling extra have certain problems in common, as employees in the actors' branch of the motion picture industry." But if extras were actors, why did it evolve that they were granted Class B membership in SAG? It was this segregation that later led to the formation of SEG.

In the July 2000 issue of the Screen Actors Guild Newsletter, the union once again attempted to define the status of extras by declaring them full-tilt actors: "One of SAG's most important mandates is securing the dignity and respect due its members as professional performers . . . In the past, the Extra was understood to be an essential ingredient in creating the entire tone, mood and atmosphere of a scene . . . These persons are performers in every sense of the word. Beginning immediately, the Guild will use the term 'Background Actor' to designate this kind of work . . . to describe more accurately the skill level and professionalism provided by our performers."

There Is a Difference

As I have pointed out throughout this book, it is important that actors in the cyber age reconnect with their shaman heritage. Actors are storytellers, and acting is an interpretative art. Extra players, while important to the moviemaking process, definitely are not actors. For SAG to designate them as such does not alter the reality of the situation, nor does it help matters. SAG's posture represents feel-good policy that is insulting to many of its trained and experienced actor members, and it cobbles the union at the labor negotiating tables. Particularly in negotiations with the advertising industry, it is difficult for SAG to demand that actors be paid as skilled professionals when, in fact, any passerby on Main Street can work as an extra and become a SAG member, no training or experience necessary. It is also a union policy that is unlikely to change. It will be, as they say, a cold day in hell before the extras once again set up their own union, and SAG is unlikely to ever again demote extras into Class B membership status.

For better or worse, SAG is now officially making up the bed each morning for both actors and extras on an equal basis, and that is that.

The question for you, the cyber-age actor, is whether or not you should work as an extra. My advice is, yes, go ahead and do it if you want to, and if your ego can handle it. But do not put the credit on your résumé because it is not considered by most people to be acting.

The arguments in favor of working as an extra are:

1. There is an educational value to it. You get to see the moviemaking process up close.
2. It is a networking opportunity for you and other aspiring actors that may be working on the movie or TV show.
3. Particularly with commercials, it can be a good day's pay.
4. There always exists the possibility that an extra will be upgraded to a principal player.

The arguments against working as an extra are:

1. Extras are frequently treated as second-class citizens on movie sets. You may hear yourself referred to as "moving furniture," and between takes, you will be ushered into a "holding pen." (I swear that is what they call the area where extras congregate!)
2. Though there is a possibility of upgrade, there is a virtual certainty that you will *not* be upgraded, particularly on a movie or TV show. Commercials are another matter because so many commercials do not have dialogue and because it is common now for producers to hire as many performers as possible as extras. They decide whom to upgrade later in the editing room.
3. Those Good Old Days when stars like Gary Cooper boasted of "starting as an extra" are gone. And, anyway, extra work is not the first rung on a ladder leading to stardom. It is not, I repeat, acting at all.
4. Extra work involves long hours and low pay, particularly in movies and TV.

The factor that concerns me the most when one of my students asks about extra work is the toll it may take on her self-esteem. It is difficult enough, in the face of constant rejection, for actors to think of themselves as leaders. The status transaction between actors and audience is one in which actors lead, and the audience follows. If you want to be cast in principal roles on a consistent basis, it is essential that you bring the dynamic of a high-status leader into the audition room. It may be more difficult to do that if yesterday you were working late into the night as a low-status extra.

Honorable and energetic people work as extras, no question about it. Occasionally, even trained and experienced actors work as extras. My stringent review of the situation is not intended to be a personal slight against anybody; I myself have worked as an extra. If you want to do it, then by all means do it. There are worse ways to spend your time, and you might make some new friends. If you do, however, remember that you are, first and foremost, an actor. If you find the experience of working as an extra demeaning the first time, definitely do not do it any more.

Compensation

It is almost impossible to believe, but the Screen Actors Guild and AFTRA, the primary performing unions, have not yet managed to negotiate even basic contracts for actors' performances distributed from the Internet. A contract was on the negotiating table for the 2000 strike against the advertising industry, but it was not the primary focus. SAG members who are attuned to the incredible developments in cyberspace can only scratch their heads in wonderment that it has taken the unions so long to get into sync with the future.

Soapbox Prediction: Digital technology, massive global audiences, television/Internet confluence, and "personal television" will make it increasingly difficult for the Screen Actors Guild and AFTRA to manage or monitor visual and audio images. It will therefore become more difficult to collect royalties or residuals on their distribution. As blasphemous as it might sound, I submit that pay-for-play, as a method of actor compensation, is an endangered concept. This arrangement, hard-won in a 1953 SAG strike, is simply not a good fit for the cyber age. Actors—and indeed all performing artists—are going to have to figure new ways of being fairly paid for their work.

The music industry is currently wrestling with these very same issues, via a truckload of lawsuits circling a small company called

Napster. Its primary business is to foster royalty-free digital copying of music, one computer user to another. Actually, the preferred high-tech term is *P2P*, which stands for "peer to peer." It may seem like a bean-brained technical distinction, but there really is a difference between sending a copy of something to umpteen million people at once versus me giving you a copy and then you giving one to your friend, "peer to peer." This is the legal argument for the defense team at Napster. Given the high price of music CDs, college kids in particular love the idea of free copies. The big music companies want royalties to be paid when copies are made. By the time you read this, the Napster case will likely be resolved. Do a search on the word Napster in a good search engine, and study it carefully if you want to see a harbinger of what awaits actors.

Once a performance of any kind, whether it is music or a movie, is converted to zeros and ones, it can be copied and transferred easily from one person to another. Making it illegal to do so will not stop the practice. The titans of the music industry will probably succeed in shutting down or emasculating Napster, but they will not succeed in shutting down the pipeline of technology. It is impossible to do so, which is my point. If negotiators for SAG and AFTRA are smart, they will not spend any more time trying to control digital duplication and distribution. They will do their actor members a favor if they focus instead on negotiating new forms of compensation instead of beating the pay-for-play drum until it breaks. There is no magic or religion in pay-for-play, and there surely are other ways for actors to profit from their work. Pay-for-play was what we needed in 1953. Today we need something else.

A possible solution is a dramatic increase—perhaps a doubling—in up-front, "buyout" compensation for performers, combined with an expansion of the wild spot arrangement. Wild spot allows unlimited airplay of a particular commercial for a thirteen-week period in predetermined markets. It will be much easier for SAG to monitor time parameters than it will be to monitor each individual airplay. Also, SAG may well ultimately restructure the kinds of productions that fall under union contract in the first place. It is very possible that the unions will at some point back away from trying to cover the lowest-budget digital productions because there are going to be too many of them, and it is not cost-effective to keep up with them all.

It pains me, a longtime union member, to say it, but our performing unions are woefully, perhaps terminally, out of step with the cyber age. They have been behind the curve since the 1980s, when cable first appeared. They were negotiating higher fees for network use when they should have been focused on cable. And now they are trying to negotiate higher fees on cable when they ought to be focusing on Internet use. By the time a new SAG contract is announced, it is almost immediately archaic. Even worse news is that it will require more than the election of a new set of SAG officers to correct this problem. It will require a blinders-off assessment of the future and the participation of a cyber-savvy membership. The union evidently considers the Internet to be just another, bigger version of network television and therefore subject to the same kinds of per-use negotiations for residual payments. It's just not so, and the sooner it comes to terms with this reality, the better off all professional actors will be.

My best guess is that the performing unions will be forced to function sort of like the insurance industry. The consumer needs major medical coverage, but he doesn't really need to have insurance policies to cover the cost of Band-Aids and aspirin. If you have open-heart surgery or an appendectomy and have to be hospitalized, or if you require treatment for a disease, you need insurance because the costs may be prohibitive. On the other hand, if you have a sore throat or a hangnail, you can probably handle the cost yourself. It is like that with actors and their jobs. We really do not need the unions to be involved in seat-of-the-pants, low-budget, and no-budget productions. State law can establish safety standards for film sets and, if salary is involved, an agent can represent the performer, or he can simply represent himself. Shamans are not children, after all.

We are likely going to see an atomic explosion of digital film production internationally. No-budget producers will understandably want to cast SAG members, and SAG members will want to accept the roles. If SAG stands in the way of these transactions, the union will self-destruct. In a way, what is coming roughly parallels the evolution of the old Showcase Code that Actors Equity developed in the late 1960s. AEA member were permitted to work for no salary in no-budget productions just as long as they were guaranteed that, if the production should move into a bigger revenue-generating situation, the actors would either go with it or be compensated for their contribution. SAG has contracts in place for the mini-budget "experimental" film, but a gusher of production will make it impractical to monitor these projects.

The performing unions will probably set a new, higher production-budget floor for movie contracts. For low-budget and no-budget projects, actors will follow accepted informal guidelines that will be widely distributed on the Internet. If you are asked to play a role in a film, the first question you ask will be, "What is the budget?" If the answer is below, say, $20,000, you will look up standard agreements online. If it is above that, you'll contact the union. There may evolve a new cottage industry for no-budget entertainment industry legal advice, to which actors can turn for guidance. With the publication and distribution of informational guidelines, probably on the Internet as well as in published books, actors at the lowest levels can fend for themselves without violating the unions' Rule Number 1, which prohibits work in nonunion productions. It is when a project has a big budget that we need the assurance that we are not being taken advantage of. Only when the budget begins to be significant is there an incentive for agents to get involved on behalf of actors.

An actor I know recently landed her first major film role. It was, of course, a digital video production. She accepted as her compensation basic expenses and per diem plus a percentage of the movie's later revenues. The producers took her to Italy and the Czech Republic for a month of shooting. The movie, if it is any good, will wind up playing in film festivals, and perhaps on down the line, it will find revenues through the Internet. The actor (not a union member yet) is comfortable with this arrangement and, indeed, feels like she is a partner in the production. If, on the other hand, she had been hired by a company with a million-dollar production budget, she would have benefited from SAG contracts. In that scenario, she likely would not receive profit participation, but her basic salary would be higher, and she would probably be represented by an agent. As it was, she represented herself, with the advice and counsel of friends and fellow professionals.

Merger

The performing unions will at some point be forced to merge. They have resisted this for more than thirty years, but push has come to shove in the cyber age. Merger between SAG and AFTRA has been voted down repeatedly by myopic union members, and nobody seems to want long-suffering Actors Equity Association at all. The digital revolution should change all of that.

For sure, there will be some very bitter labor conflicts before these matters of compensation and distribution of the consumer box-office dollars are resolved. At this moment, a few enormous multinational companies are holding all the aces in the deck, and they're doing their level best to prevent any reshuffling and dealing of new hands. Their efforts will fail because there is no turning back the progress of cyber-age technology. The evolution of cyberspace is very much like the evolution of appliances back when electricity was first harnessed. It was not an option then to shut off the electricity just so the candle makers could thrive, and there is not an option now of shutting off the Internet so that old-school movie studios and television networks can thrive. We are steadily heading toward the day when all of recorded entertainment will wind up as zeros and ones spinning through cyber-space, reaching a new global audience.

New actors today are poised to be pioneers and trailblazers in a way that actors have not been for a hundred years. It is an exciting time to be a shaman.

Appendix

Websites

www.actorsite.com/
A Hollywood-based website that features a ton of local resources, including a map to audition sites, descriptions of current television shows, and a website-hosting service.

www.showfax.com/
A division of Breakdown Services in Hollywood. A subscription to ShowFax permits you to download scripts and sides into your computer.

www.breakdownservices.com
Breakdown Services provides a number of services, including up-to-date lists of Hollywood agents and casting directors.

www.variety.com
Daily Variety is one of the two major Hollywood trade papers.

www.hollywoodreporter.com
Hollywood Reporter is the other major Hollywood trade paper.

www.backstagecasting.com
Backstage West/DramaLogue is the primary actor-oriented trade paper in Hollywood.

www.theatermania.com
Provides theatrical news, reviews, and gossip.

www.aint-it-cool-news.com
Provides film industry news, past, present, and future.

www.edhooks.com
My personal website. Come up and see me some time.

www.iFilm.com
A Cyberplex. Here, you can download and watch more than 1,400 short movies.

www.atomfilms.com
Another Cyberplex that features digital films, both live-action and animation.

www.imdb.com
A huge database of film and television credits. If you want a list of Strother Martin's credits, this is the place to go.

www.sag.com/
The official website for Screen Actors Guild.

www.aftra.org/
The official website for the American Federation of Television and Radio Artists (AFTRA).

www.actorsequity.org
The official website for Actors Equity Association (AEA).

Works Cited

American Theatre. 2000. "The Field and Its Challenges." Reported by Stephanie Coen with Stephen C. Forman and Ben Cameron. January.

Barlow, John Perry. 1995. "Is There a There There in Cyberspace?" *Utne Reader*.

———. 2000. "The Next Economy of Ideas." *Wired* (October).

Brook, Peter. 1968. *The Empty Space*. New York: Touchstone Books/Simon & Schuster.

———. 1987. *The Shifting Point*. New York: Theatre Communications Group.

———. 1995. *The Open Door*. New York: Theatre Communications Group.

Caine, Michael. 1997. *Acting in Film: An Actor's Take on Movie Making*. New York: Applause Theatre Books.

Carnicke, Sharon M. 1998. *Stanislavsky in Focus*. Newark, NJ: Harwood Academic Publishers.

Chaikin, Joseph. 1972. *The Presence of the Actor*. New York: Theatre Communications Group.

Daily Variety. 2000. "Survey Predicts Big Jump in 'Net Ad Revs." Reported by Tim Swanson, 17 August.

Ekman, Paul, and M. O'Sullivan. 1991. "Facial Expression: Methods, Means, and Moues." In *Fundamentals of Nonverbal Behavior*, edited by R. S. Feldman and B. Rime. New York: Cambridge University Press.

Ekman, Paul, Robert W. Levenson, and Wallace V. Friesen. 1983. "Autonomic Nervous Systems Activity Distinguishes Among Emotions." *Science* 221 (September): 1208–10.

Esslin, Martin. 1976. *An Anatomy of Drama*. London: Abacus.

Guare, John. 1990. *Six Degrees of Separation*. New York: Dramatists Play Service.

Hooks, Ed. 2000a. *Acting for Animators*. Portsmouth, NH: Heinemann.

————. 2000b. *The Audition Book: Winning Strategies for Breaking into Theater, Film, and TV.* 3d edition. New York: Backstage Books.

Hozlowski, Rob. 2000. *The Actor's Guide to the Internet.* Portsmouth, NH: Heinemann.

Kirby, Ernest Theodore. 1975. *Ur-Drama: The Origins of Theatre.* New York: New York University Press.

Longo, Oddone. 1990. "The Theater of the Polis." In *Nothing to Do with Dioynsos? Athenian Drama in Its Social Context,* edited by John J. Winkler and Froma I. Zeitlin, 12–19. Princeton, NJ: Princeton University Press.

Lutz, Tom. 1999. *Crying: The Natural and Cultural History of Tears.* New York: W. W. Norton.

Mamet, David. 1999. *True and False: Heresy and Common Sense for the Actor.* New York: Vintage Books/Random House.

Meisner, Sanford, and Dennis Longwell. 1987. *Sanford Meisner on Acting.* New York: Vintage Books.

Menache, Alberto. 2000. *Understanding Motion Capture for Computer Animation and Video Games.* San Francisco: Morgan Kaufmann/Academic Press.

New York Times. 2000. "More Vehemently Than Ever, Europe Is Scorning the U.S." Reported by Susanne Daley, 9 April, international edition.

New York Times. 2000. "Low-Price, Highly Ambitious Digital Chip." Reported by Andrew Ross Sorkin, 11 September.

New York Times. 2000. "Behind the Wheel and Driving the Nation's Culture." 17 September.

Ogilvy, David. 1987. *Ogilvy on Advertising.* New York: Random House.

San Francisco Examiner. 2000. "Smart Move Leads Back to Broadway." Reported by Douglas J. Rowe, 19 August.

San Jose Mercury News. 2000. "Still Stage Struck." Reported by Karen D'Souza, 2 July.

San Jose Mercury News. 2000. "Digital Scene Stealers." Reported by Robert Philpot, 31 August.

San Jose Mercury News. 2000. "Internet Now Has More International Appeal." 2 September.

Screen Actors Guild Newsletter. 2000 (July).

Silverberg, Larry. 1994. *The Sanford Meisner Approach*. Smith and Kraus.

Stanislavsky, Constantin. 1936. *An Actor Prepares*. Translated. New York: Theatre Arts Books. Reprint edition, June 1989.

―――. 1950. *Building a Character*. Translated. New York: Theatre Arts Books. Reprint edition, June 1989.

―――. 1952. *My Life in Art*. Translated. New York: Theatre Arts Books. Reprint edition, October 1987.

―――. 1961. *Creating a Role*. Translated. New York: Theatre Arts Books. Reprint edition, June 1989.

Strasberg, Lee. 1965. *Strasberg at the Actors Studio*. Edited by Robert H. Hethmon, 115–16. New York: Theatre Communications Group.

Wright, Robert. 1994. *The Moral Animal*. New York: Pantheon Books/Random House.